THE TORN TUNIC

Tito Casini

THE TORN TUNIC

Letter of a Catholic on the "liturgical Reform"

Foreword by
Antonio Cardinal Bacci

Preface by
Thomas Cattoi

Angelico Press

CATHOLIC
TRADITIONALIST
CLASSICS

Cover design
by Michael Schrauzer

CONTENTS

Part II

IN GRATIA CANTANTES DEO

Appendix

PREFACE TO THE
ANGELICO PRESS EDITION (2020)

The Chiesa di Ognissanti (Church of All Saints) on the Via Appia Nuova is not one of Rome's countless tourist magnets. Run by the Sons of Divine Providence (FDP) founded by Saint Luigi Orione (1872–1940), the parish was established in the early twentieth century to serve the needs of the working class population around the Porta San Giovanni. On March 7th, 1965—the first Sunday of Lent—Pope Paul VI celebrated Mass at the Chiesa di Ognissanti in the course of his visit to the parish. Ordinarily, such an event would have attracted only local interest; bishops of Rome routinely visit parishes scattered around the Eternal City as part of their pastoral duties. This occasion, however, was different, as a plaque in Italian—repeatedly vandalized and replaced—informs visitors to the church to this day:

> On March 7th, 1965, His Holiness Paul VI, inaugurating the liturgical reform decreed by the Second Ecumenical Vatican Council, deigned to celebrate in this temple the first Mass in the Italian language, amidst the emotion and joy of an entire people, forever faithful and grateful.

This event, which actually took place four years before the promulgation of the *Novus Ordo Missae*, marked the first occasion in history when a Roman Pontiff celebrated Mass publicly in any language other than Latin. The rite used on that day was the so-called "1965 Missal," which was essentially the 1962 Missal promulgated by John XXIII with the modernizations and simplifications laid out by the Instruction *Inter Oecumenici*, published on September 26th, 1964, and coming into effect on the very day of Pope Paul's pastoral visit to the Chiesa di Ognissanti. In fact, despite the plaque's bombastic claim, the Mass would not have been entirely in Italian, since *Inter Oecumenici* expressly mandated that the Orations, the Preface, and the Roman Canon were to remain in Latin—and, in fact, the Canon continued to be read silently.

The impact of this event, however, could hardly be overstated. For the first time, a bishop of Rome celebrated the Eucharist using the vernacular, with greatly simplified rubrics and ceremonies. What is more, he chose to do so on a hastily arranged makeshift altar, facing the people. Only three years had gone by since February 22nd, 1962, when, a few months before the opening of the Council, John XXIII had promulgated the Apostolic Constitution *Veterum Sapientia*, in which he extolled the role of the Latin language in preserving and transmitting the deposit of the Catholic Faith, and earnestly recommended that it be preserved as the sole language of worship and even of theological instruction.

Of course, the dismantling of the immemorial Roman Rite had begun in earnest, and would only gather speed over the course of the following years. *Sacrosanctum Concilium* had been approved on December 4th, 1963, and the Advisory Body for the Implementation of the Constitution on the Liturgy (Consilium ad exsequendam Constitutionem liturgicam) had been established on January 25th, 1964. Pope Paul appointed the Vicentian Father Annibale Bugnini (1912–1982) to be the secretary of this body, which would draft the *Novus Ordo Missae* that would *de facto* replace the 1962 Missal from the first Sunday of Advent in 1969. Bugnini would remain secretary of the Consilium until 1975, but until 1967 its president was Cardinal Giacomo Lercaro (1891–1976), Archbishop of Bologna and one of the leading "progressive" figures in the Italian church.

If Cardinal Giuseppe Siri (1906-89), who was Archbishop of Genoa from 1946 until 1987, was the figure of reference for the more conservative wing of Italian Catholicism, Lercaro was an outspoken reformist, who was not afraid to speak his mind not only on all manner of ecclesial issues, but on social and political issues as well.

Indeed, it was his sermon on January 1st, 1968, attacking the US bombing of Vietnam, that led to his eventual fall from grace and his removal from the See of Bologna and other positions within the Curia. Lercaro was always in broad agreement with Bugnini's push for vernacularization and a drastic simplifications of the liturgical books; while he did play a lesser role in the actual drafting of the new missal than many people thought at the time, for a few years immediately after the end of the Council he was by far the most visible representative of the body overseeing the implementation of the liturgical reform.

The council had ended on December 8th, 1965, and soon after that, on February 5th, 1966, the Italian writer Cristina Campo (1923–1977) submitted a petition to Paul VI signed by thirty-seven international artists and intellectuals, asking the Pope to make sure that at least monastic houses would preserve the Latin liturgy and the use of Gregorian chant. This petition may have played a role in convincing the Pope to issue the Apostolic Letter *Sacrificium Laudis*, which emphasized the importance of maintaining the traditional form of the Divine Office for the vitality of monasticism. On June 7th, 1966, the same Cristina Campo, together with Duke Filippo Caffarelli and the Nobel Prize-winner Eugenio Montale, establish the first Italian section of the international organization *Una Voce*, an international association based in Zurich whose goal was (and remains today) the preservation of the Latin liturgy. The years following the Council are characterized both by a marked uncertainty as to the actual future shape of the liturgy and by a growing activism on the part of prominent cultural figures in Italy as well as in other European countries.

The Torn Tunic (*La tunica strappata*) by Tito Casini (1897–1987) is one of the most representative and significant works penned during the immediate aftermath of Vatican II. The introduction by the author is dated February 22nd, 1967, the Feast of the Chair of Saint Peter, and the fifth anniversary of the already mentioned *Veterum Sapientia*. Casini addresses his *cri de cœur* to Cardinal Lercaro, albeit without naming him explicitly—though hardly any Italian reader of the time would have been in doubt as to the identity of the recipient. At the same time, Casini was addressing the Italian church as a whole, and indeed, he was hoping to attract the attention of Pope Paul himself, whose document *Sacrificium Laudis*, honored more in the breach than in the observance, was actually included in the appendix of the Italian edition and its later translation. Casini is not deploring the introduction of the *Novus Ordo Missae*, or engaging in extensive comparisons between the new Missal and the Gregorian liturgy last codified by John XXIII; he is not doing that because the Novus Ordo was yet to come, and the work of the Consilium was not yet complete. At the time of this work's publication, practicing Catholics had experienced no more than three to four years of liturgical innovation, and had a very clear memory of the pre-conciliar liturgical practices that many of them had been attending for decades. As such, Casini's argument reflects a very specific time and place, a point at which the actual scale and the long-term impact of the liturgical reform were yet to unfold; even more importantly, perhaps, a point at which the episcopal *trahison des clercs* that would try to push the traditional liturgical books into oblivion was yet to come.

Casini was able to get the support of a prominent curial official, Cardinal Antonio Bacci (1885–1971), who had strongly opposed the introduction of the vernacular into the liturgy and who was known for the publication of a *Lexicon Eorum Vocabulorum Quae Difficilius Latine Redduntur*, a Latin dictionary of contemporary terms. A few years later, in September 1969, Bacci, together with Cardinal Ottaviani and a group of Roman theologians and writers that again included Cristina Campo, were to author the Ottaviani intervention, which cast serious doubt on the Catholic orthodoxy of the new Missal of Paul VI. In early 1967, however, it was as yet impossible to foresee to what degree the new Missal would distance itself from the older liturgical books. Casini's intervention was motivated by the hope that the Council's own injunctions about the preservation of Latin and Gregorian chant would actually be heeded, and that the liturgical chaos of the previous three to four years would eventually be regarded as an aberration—an aberration due to the weakness of the Church's own pastors, to whose conscience Casini was now appealing. Indeed, Casini clearly holds Pope Paul responsible for this state of affairs, often referring to the Pope's first celebration of the Mass in Italian on March 7th, 1965 as the moment when all defenses broke down, a symbolic rupture with the tradition that in his view could only have tragic consequences.

Who was Tito Casini? Thirty-three years after his death, even in his native Italy, few remember his work. Most of his novels, essays, and short stories are out of print, and his name is unknown even to most scholars of twentieth-century Italian literature. Casini was born in 1897 in the village of Cornacchia, near Firenzuola, in the region of Tuscany. He was in many ways a Tuscan writer even more than an Italian one: someone whose intellectual horizon and imagination is profoundly shaped by the landscape and history of his native land, whose hills are dotted with beautiful churches and monasteries, and whose towns—Florence, Siena, Pisa, but also the innumerable small *borghi* scattered from the Apennines to the Tyrrenian sea—almost allow us to touch with our own hands the great artistic and cultural legacy of medieval Christendom. Far from the commercial hub of Milan, but also removed from the center of political and ecclesial life in Rome, Florence in the early twentieth century but also in the interwar period was a lively center of literary and artistic activity. Casini was a friend or a colleague of many of the leading figure of the Tuscan literary renaissance of those years, such as Giovanni Papini (1881–1956), Nicola Lisi (1893–1975), Carlo Betocchi (1899–1986), who was born in Turin but spent his most important creative years in Florence, and Piero Bargellini (1897–1980), who would later embark on a political career and was Major of Florence during the catastrophic flood of 1966. Together with Papini and Lisi, Casini was one of the founders and leading contributors to the journal *Il Frontespizio* (*The Frontispiece* or *The Title-Page*), which from 1929 until the cessation of its publication in 1940 due to the outbreak of World War II was one of the leading publications on the Italian literary scene. Under the supervision of Father Giuseppe de Luca, the goal of the *Frontespizio* was to offer a venue for Catholic writers who wanted to retain a measure of independence from the Fascist regime, but were also opposed to Marxism or literary avant-gardism and futurism. Its embrace of a non-political Catholic traditionalism meant that many of its authors were very critical of the Italian Church hierarchy, whose enthusiastic attitude towards the regime—especially after the 1929 Lateran Concordate between the Vatican and the Italian state—left little room for dissent. Many of Casini's initial writings appeared in the *Frontespizio*, but were published again independently after the war, at a time when the Italian literary establishment had veered strongly to the left and a "local" Catholic perspective like that of this journal was increasingly dismissed as reactionary and irrelevant.

Casini's essays are often acerbic, even as his harshness is moderated by an elegiac attachment to the traditions of rural Tuscany, traditions already disappearing in the 1950s and 1960s under the pressure of modernization. The penchant for invective had a long tradition in the region; even Dante Alighieri, after all, was far from tender with his enemies in the *Commedia*, which Casini is fond of quoting in *The Torn Tunic*. In the 19th century, Carlo Lorenzini (1826–1890), better known as Carlo Collodi, did not just author the children's novel everyone remembers as *Pinocchio*, but was actually better known for his satirical writings and exposés of political corruption and mediocrity in post-reunification Italy. Casini is a writer very much in Collodi's vein: an often anti-clerical Catholic, very willing to call out the hierarchy for its mistakes. At the same time, he is also a very "classical" author, who, like Dante, has a great admiration for Virgil, the Latin poet who takes Alighieri through the circles of hell, but who also authored elegiac descriptions of rural life, the *Eclogues* and the *Georgics*. Casini authored a number of essays on Virgil, and some of his narrative works—*Il Pane sotto la Neve* (*The Bread under the Snow*), *I Giorni del Ciliegio* (*The Days of the Cherry Tree*), *I Giorni del Castagno* (*The*

Days of the Chestnut Tree) reflect a Catholic as well as a classical sensitivity that invests the life of traditional Italian peasants with an almost sacred quality. American readers will perhaps remember Ermanno Olmi's movie *The Tree of Wooden Clogs* (1978) as a cinematic articulation of this particular vision.

When Casini writes *The Torn Tunic*, however, the days of *Il Frontespizio* are long behind him. By the 1960s, he is already a marginal figure—certainly not a part of the Italian literary establishment, which in those years was enthusiastically embracing the nihilism of the novels by Alberto Moravia (1907–1990) or even the very different kind of Catholicism permeating the work of Pier Paolo Pasolini (1922–1975). Casini's book is almost a *succès de scandale*, and many bishops ordered that it be withdrawn from Catholic bookstores. Translations into numerous European languages, usually abridged and eliminating many references of interest to Italian readers alone, quickly followed.

Did Casini accomplish what he had hoped to accomplish? If we consider what happened over the following few years, his words of warning clearly went unheeded. Casini, however, was not one to be easily discouraged, and as we see from his later writings, he was convinced that his view would eventually prevail. Again, as a Tuscan, he was looking back at the history of his land, and there he found reasons to hope. In 1786, in the city of Pistoia, Bishop Scipione Ricci (1741–1810), with the support of Grand-Duke Leopold of Tuscany, called a diocesan synod to reform the liturgical and devotional life of his church. The synod, which was supposed to pave the way for a "national" Tuscan synod extending to the whole of the Grand-duchy, voted for the translation of the Roman liturgical books into the vernacular, and also called for other reforms, such as the suppression of side altars and the drastic simplification of the Divine Office. Interestingly enough, as Casini mentions in passing in the *Torn Tunic*, the local populace and the peasantry were appalled at these developments and vociferously called for the restoration of traditional practices. Eventually, in 1794, Pope Pius VI condemned the decisions of the Synod of Pistoia with the Bull *Auctorem Fidei*. Many years later,

Casini's widow would recount the conversations that her husband had with Cristina Campo—herself a Florentine transplant to Rome—about the current situation of the liturgy and the Church. Both Campo and Casini hoped that a future pontiff, perhaps already Montini's successor, would make a decisive intervention like that of Pius VI and undo the decisions of Bugnini's committee.

It is interesting to observe that for Casini, the battle for the defense of the traditional liturgy was a battle that had to be fought by the laity and for the laity, whom the reform was depriving of access to centuries of Catholic tradition. Casini was familiar with the tract *Le Cinque Piaghe della Santa Chiesa* (*The Five Wounds of the Holy Church*), authored in 1832 by the priest Antonio Rosmini (1797–1855). In this work, Rosmini foregrounded five major obstacles to Church reform in the first part of the nineteenth century. The first such 'wound' was the fact that the laity could not understand the liturgy. Some reformers of the 1960s were fond of claiming that they had finally addressed Rosmini's concern, but Casini forcefully pointed out that Rosmini was not asking for the traditional liturgy to be eliminated and replaced by a new one, but for the laity to be provided with translations or in general to be better educated. Indeed, in his view, the true defenders of the laity's rights were those who supported the preservation of the traditional liturgical books.

Towards the end of his life, the tone of Casini's writings grew more apocalyptic, without however losing hope that one day the situation in the Church and in the world would change. In 1976, he authored another pamphlet, *Nel Fumo di Satana: Verso l'Ultimo Scontro* (*Within Satan's Smoke: Towards the Last Battle*), where he affirmed his faith that, one day, the traditional Mass would be restored:

> It will rise again, I tell you, [...] the Mass will rise again, as I tell so many who come to complain (and sometimes they cry as they do so); and to him who asks me how I can be so sure of it, I answer (as a poet, if you would like) bringing him to my balcony and showing him the sun... It will be evening soon,

but [...] the sun will rise again; it will shine again after the night, to brighten up the earth from the sky, because...because it is the sun, and God established it for our life and comfort. Thus, I add, it is, and thus it will be with the Mass—the Mass which is "ours," Catholic, of all times, and of all people: our spiritual sun so beautiful, so holy, and so sanctifying—against the delusion of the bats, driven out of their hiding places by the reform, who believe that their hour—the hour of darkness—will not end.

Thomas Cattoi
Graduate Theological Union
Berkeley, CA

TRANSLATOR'S INTRODUCTORY NOTE

Copies of this little book first appeared in the bookshops of Rome in March this year. It was described in the Italian press as a literary atomic bomb, or pyrobulus atomicus, term found in the Italian-Latin dictionary of modern words by Cardinal Bacci, the Church's greatest Latinist, who has served four popes in the drawing up of major official documents.

Almost at once, the first printing sold out. La Tunica Stracciata, now in its sixth edition, has since gone all over the world, having been translated into French and German (with Spanish to come) besides English.

Esteemed by Pius XII and by John XXIII, Tito Casini has given a number of works to Italian literature, best known among which are his four books on the Georgic and liturgical seasons, which for their skilful interweaving of themes from the Missal *and the* Georgics *have been called the « Christian Virgil. » His last work, a two-volume novel entitled* Maremma amara, *gained a 1966 literary award. Now he has been moved to take up his pen in defence of the Roman liturgy against those he considers mainly responsible for the ousting of Latin and the replacing of it with «reformed » vernacular rites.*

A word about the English text here offered:
dissertations on the ugliness, inadequacy and ab-
surdities of the Italian vernacular have been short-
ened or cut, as have a few other passages of purely
local reference; but new material added for this
edition has been incorporated.

Inspite of every care to remain otherwise as
perfectly faithful as possible to both the spirit and
the letter of this book, some of the peculiar raciness
of the writer's highly colloquial but classical Flo-
rentine will inevitably have been reduced — his
« gusts of pure mountain air » transformed into
rather gentler but (it is hoped) no less invigorating
sea breezes.

Rome, September 8th 1967

FOREWORD

I have been asked to write a brief foreword to this little book by Tito Casini. I cannot — neither do I wish to — refuse. Indeed, I do so gladly, although not without some reserve.

I consider Tito Casini, whom I have known since boyhood, one of the first Catholic writers of Italy. His style — fresh, frank and caustic — is like a gust of the pure mountain air one breathes in his beloved Florence — his and mine. Casini is a Christian all of one piece, and can well say, with the ancient writer: « Christianus mihi nomen, catholicus cognomen: *Christian I am called, and Catholic is my name.* » *And if what he has here set down may seem to some too little reverent, all will be bound to admit it was dictated solely by his passionate love for the Church, and her liturgical decorum. In any case, it may and must be affirmed, that what Casini says in this little volume never goes contrary to what has been laid down in the second Vatican Council's Constitution on the Liturgy. What it impugns is an* application *of this Constitution in practice which certain frenzied and fanatical innovators have been seeking at all costs to impose. And it is beyond words what some are doing by this slippery programme with their so-called Eucharistic suppers, pop-masses, beatle-masses, yè-yè-masses and suchlike obscenities.*

I am very glad, I say, to write this foreword, as I think these pages that put one in mind of the still more fiery, bold and forthright ones of St. Catherine of Siena will be able to right certain ideas and be of good service.

I feel sure, meanwhile, that those concerned will freely forgive the author certain expressions that may appear little respectful in their regard, reflecting they were not penned with the intention of giving offence but from a mind and heart exasperated by some of these innovations, which seem, and are, utter profanations.

We all, for that matter, have continually something to learn — even from the view of lay people — and especially from such laymen, as Tito Casini, who are model Catholics.

And here I must at least remind the reader that an international federation has been set up for the safeguarding of Latin and Gregorian chant in the Catholic liturgy. This federation now numbers hosts of persons of all ranks in fourteen nations, with headquarters at Zurich, Switzerland. A review is published called UNA VOCE — Latin for with one voice — the words being identical in Italian, and not so different from the English! Italian is almost a dialect of Latin, and the Latin of the liturgy, which is heir to the sermo rusticus, the rustic discourse of the people, is easily understandable to the greater part of them — perhaps better understood than some of these barbaric vernacular versions. If the same cannot be said of English, the average English-speaking Catholic in all parts of the world can still at least understand enough of the general meaning to perceive the advantage of Latin over texts that are more a betrayal of the true and original words and phrases than a translation.

In this year's January bulletin, Italian UNA VOCE expressed what it feels a duty to denounce as a predicament « not in the least in harmony with the renewal hoped for by the Council. » The Constitution on the Liturgy, in article 36, lays down as a general principle that Latin shall be maintained in sacred rites, whilst granting the use of the common speech in the Lessons and certain determined parts of the Mass if thought to serve the people's better understanding. But the total and indiscriminate use of the vernacular, as practised in many parts of Italy and other countries, is not only contrary to the Council, but the cause, too, of intense spiritual suffering for large numbers of people.

I therefore think that the petition sent by UNA VOCE international association for the safeguarding of Latin and sacred music in the Catholic liturgy to the national Episcopal Conference is deserving of careful and favourable consideration. For, with the celebration of the Mass and other rites in bad Italian and national languages, or Esperanto, Latin, the Church's official language, would risk being totally barred, like a dangerous animal.

It seems opportune, then, at least in cathedral churches, sanctuaries and tourist centres, and everywhere that enough priests are to be found, for a certain number of Latin Masses to be celebrated, at fixed times, to meet the just desires of all, whatever their nationality, who prefer Latin to the vernacular, and Gregorian chant to the mean and trivial type of popular ditty that is today attempting to oust it, with assuredly little benefit to the seemliness of Catholic worship.

✠ ANTONIO Cardinal BACCI
(Vatican City, February 23rd 1967)

INTRODUCTION

This « letter », written in a style so different from my usual one, as readers of other works of mine will know, was put away for months in a drawer. It was extremely bold and I kept on hoping and hesitating — hoping that acknowledgement of mistakes on the part of certain authorities, and the following of better counsel, would give me joyful cause to tear up as no longer needed what had cost me such pain to compose.

But no: the Catholic liturgy continued to be attacked — and is still being attacked — in its forms, language and song — by a band of innovators or « progressives », in reality as antiquated and behind the times as the Bishop of Pistoia and Grand Duke Leopold (*). It should therefore be no cause for amazement that, in defence of the Spouse of Christ, Whose beauty I have hitherto endeavoured to celebrate with constant love, I now exchange my pen for a sword. Fortis est ut mors dilectio, dura sicut infernus aemulatio.

At length, in the summer of 1966, these pages went to press — only to be withdrawn by me on reading with great rejoicing the Holy Father's Apo-

---

(*) The Acts of the Synod of Pistoia, convened by the Bishop in 1786 under the influence of Leopold of Tuscany, were condemned as contrary to Catholic practice and papal authority by Pius VI in 1794 by the Bull Auctorem Fidei.

*stolic Letter, dated August 15th, Feast of the As-
sumption,* Sacrificium laudis, *repudiating with
such force and persuasion the pretensions and acti-
vities of Modernism in respect to the Divine Office*: « *It has come to Our notice (the Holy Father
wrote) that vernacular tongues are being demanded
for the chanting of the Office in choir and that
efforts are being made here and there to replace
the chant known as Gregorian with the type of popular ditty in vogue today; moreover, that some are
actually claiming that Latin be abolished. We are
bound to admit that demands of this kind have
caused Us grave disquiet and no little sadness; and
the question arises whence this frame of mind,
and formerly unheard of insufferance, comes, and
why it has spread...* » *After recalling what was laid
down by the Constitution on the Liturgy, clearly
averse to such a way of thinking, the Pope goes
on*: « *Nor is it only a matter of conserving the Latin
language — language that, far from deserving small
honour, is certainly worthy of being energetically
defended as the most fertile source, in the Latin
Church, of Christian civilisation and as the richest
treasury of pious devotion; it is also a matter of
keeping intact the proper form, beauty and original
vigour of these prayers and chants... It therefore
causes astonishment that this manner of praying,
disturbed by the sudden commotion, can now seem
to some negligible.* » *Having next confuted an
inconsistent objection in regard to Latin, the Pope's
Letter continues*: « *The choir deprived of that
language which is above the boundaries of individual nations and whose worth is in its wonderful
spiritual force, the choir that were to eliminate
those melodies that spring from the depths of the
soul — Gregorian chant, We mean — would be like a
snuffed candle, giving light no more, no more drawing men's minds and eyes... We have no wish* » *(the*

Apostolic Letter ends, adding force to the confutation) « *for the love that We bear you and the great esteem that is Ours, to grant what could cause a worsening, and be the origin, may be, of no small harm to yourselves, as well as of the undoubted weakening and sorrow of the whole Church of God. Allow Us to protect your heritage, even inspite of yourselves.* » (*)

There was, in this, reason for rejoicing and hope — but what, in actual fact, happened? At the Liturgical Week *held a bare fortnight after the Holy Father's Letter, a programme was launched widening the field for the vernacular and modern popular songs, including among others these items: preparation of a translation of the Psalms, of official character, for use at Vespers and divine service; revision and adaptation in the national language of the rite of Eucharistic Benediction (and we were given a foretaste of the quality of such adaptation); preparation of a translation of the Gradual and melodies for texts in the vernacular; translation,to become official, of the common prayers used throughout the nation, such as the* Angelus Domini, *the Litany of Loreto, and so on, and so on — all, as can be seen, clearly according with the Holy Father's Letter, as black with white.*

So back went my manuscript to the printers — where it however remained, in yet further hope and hesitation, until the autumn and the still greater vandalistic assault which was stemmed by the Pope *in his allocution of October 13th reminding the members of the Consilium for the carrying out of the liturgical Constitution of the* « *sense of the sacred that demands reverence for such ceremonies as the Church has ordained for divine wor-*

(*) *Paul VI's Apostolic Letter* Sacrificium laudis *is printed in full as an appendix.*

ship, *of the respect for tradition by means of which* a precious and venerated heritage is given Us, *and condemning the iconoclastic fury* (festinatione quasi iconoclastarum) *which would reform and change everything...*

The assault was still being made. Therefore, all hesitation at an end, and availing myself of the « liberty, even the duty » *recognised and instilled by the Council in the laity's regard (liberty denied by the Consilium)* of speaking up « on what concerns the Church's well-being » (*Constitution* De Ecclesia) *I at last decided there was nothing now to stop this little book from being issued.*

With what hopes in mind? Let me reply: with none whatever in men, all whatever in Him Whose soldiers we became in Confirmation. Obliged to fight like partisans — and possibly with a partisan's intemperance — I call to mind the words of a great partisan of God (though disproportionate the comparison) Matathias to his sons when dying: « *Now pride and subversion prevail. Therefore, my sons, be zealous and firm in the faith!...* »

Armed with faith, we are fighting and shall fight for Israel within Israel — for the Church within the Church — recollecting Christ's saying: « non veni pacem mittere sed gladium — *I came not to bring peace but a sword* », offering to God *the grief, too, of being constrained to war against* ″ enemies ″ *who are in reality beloved brothers, whether laymen such as I, or Churchmen such as the eminent personage to whom this* « letter » *is addressed, for the sake of propriety not referred to by name.*

TITO CASINI

(Florence, February 22nd 1967, Feast of St. Peter's Chair, 5th anniversary of the Apostolic Constitution, Veterum Sapientia).

"UNANIMES UNO ORE"

Your Eminence —

I thought of you the other day on reading in the *Osservatore Romano* of something that happened thirty years or so ago. I was moved to think of you, let me tell you at the outset, in a certain context and in regard to a particular day — March 7th 1965 — memorable in the Church's history. You already know my views about this, so will not be surprised.

The episode took place in Rome, on September 11th 1932, to be precise, during the demolition work ordered by Mussolini for the opening up of the new road known as the *via dei Fori Imperiali*. Among the victims was a church, St. Mary *in Macello Martyrum*, dear to a multitude both for its age and religious associations — not, however, looked upon as sufficiently weighty a consideration to prevent demolition. The moment came for

1

knocking down the wall with a much-venerated fresco of the Crucifixion, and permission to proceed was asked of the commission present, made up of a number of artists and a Bishop. Permission given — the painting being of paltry artistic worth — the Bishop with a « turn of the thumb » signed a workman to begin demolition of the wall.

With marked reluctance, which he made no attempt to conceal, the man took up his pick-axe, but remained without raising it, hesitant, until, turning to the Bishop whom he possibly took for an ordinary member of the clergy, he exclaimed: « Your Reverence, I am a Christian. I don't feel I can do it... If you really want this, at least will you yourself strike the first blows? » His Lordship reddened. No one spoke a word. But all eyes turned again to the fresco... Then there *was* something to be said for it, after all... The painting was spared.

I do not know — the writer does not say — who that Bishop was. But I am sure it could not have been you; for if it had been, you would have acted on the workman's suggestion and, with « symbolic » meaning in your gesture, have lent a willing hand in the destruction of that antiquated and « non-functional » church, despite its appeal to the « esthetes » and its ancient associations for the people.

Such an act of destruction you have succeeded in effecting, with strenuous efforts and with the help, we know, of others, on an incomparably wider scale and with far more shameful havoc, by your March 7th 1965.

I am not referring, your Eminence, to the way opened up by your pick-axe blows and declarations for the removal and destruction that is still going on in church after church of altars, tabernacles, Communion rails, statues, pulpits, friezes and art-works

fashioned and set up in the course of centuries
to the glory and the service of the faith; it is not
churches and church buildings only I am thinking
of, but *the Church* — Mother Church, holy and
beautiful — to which I belong as you do, and which
belongs to me, as well as she does to you: whence
my right and duty to employ my pen, raise this
voice of mine, for her, displeased if this displease
you, no less resolute all the same.

But can this really displease you? Can it truly
displease you, or make you wonder, that someone
— a layman — speaks out what he really thinks,
in matters of religion, to a member of the clergy,
a Bishop as you are, and a Cardinal in addition?
Without reminding you that when prophets are
found wanting God can make use of an ass, give
faculty of speech to an ass for admonishing them
(and I wish you the humility of Balaam in my regard) I make appeal to my status as a layman in
doing precisely what might, on second thoughts,
have seemed, even to me, daring, however rightly
intended. You mitred Pastors have so cajoled and
encouraged us hitherto simple lambs of the flock
entrusted to Peter on the shores of Galilee that to
some you appear to have been overdoing it, so that
the joke went round of the up-dated encyclopedia
in which the term « laity » would most likely be
given as see *clergy*, and « clergy » as see *laity*.

Joking apart, you have attributed so much importance to us in the running of the Church's
affairs — I appeal to your Eminence's own words
telecast three days before March 7th 1965: « Certainly this Council may be called the Council of
the laity » — you have spoken such a great deal
about this, so inebriated us with the idea of « liberty », as to make it seem no longer irreverent to be
outspoken in the Church — so then why not to
you?

THE « SENSUS FIDELIUM »

It is comforting, furthermore, to be able to find an example of a layman's having thus spoken out in the Church, in regard to Churchmen — and Churchmen from the lowest to the highest rank of ecclesiastical dignity — with a « liberty » never before and never since known: a layman whom the Council has extolled, for his faith, as the Church's most profound and sublime poet-apologist. I mean Dante, your Eminence. Dante, whom your confrères in the Episcopate honoured by coming in such numbers during the Council from Rome to Florence: Dante, whom the popes have lauded and fêted — Paul VI on behalf of them all by dedicating to him amongst other things the *motu proprio Altissimi cantus*, which does not pass over, but praises, as a mark of his zeal and vehement filial love of the Church, the invectives against Churchmen who in his eyes were doing her no honour (« *officium iudicis et correctoris, quod sibi vindicat, ipsi conciliat, praesertim cum lamentabilia vitia carpit...* »)

Apropos of the things that have induced me, your Eminence, to address this « letter » to you, a well-known theologian (whom for his peace I do not name) has affirmed in « *Crie de Coeur of a Christian* » that, faced with certain deviations on the part of Bishops, « the worst of evils would be for the flock to show supine acquiescence and follow them. » He quotes instances of lay people who have in the past openly and clamorously rebelled, with scandal, whom the Church has afterwards declared saints. He recalls the « *sensus fidelium* », that feeling for the faith that roused Christians to sound the alarm against the novelties of Arius and Nestorius, and the words of St. Hilary, hammer of the Arians: « The ears of the faithful are more Catholic than the mouths of certain Bishops. »

We believe, your Eminence (I say we, and not I, for we are a goodly number) that it has now come to this, and that we have therefore to make it our duty to cry the alarm, and put up resistance. And if it comes about that, with you, we do it too roughly — if my pen should happen to run away with me from sheer indignation — I find some justification in your particular regard remembering the words uttered on one occasion by Pius XI to a confrère of yours, the Bishop of Camerino: « St. Ignatius, who knew something of the passions, has a magnificent chapter in which he says that every human passion should be kept down but a little allowed to remain of irascability » to which the Bishop replied (and I make his hope my own): « Please God, if I have been too high-spirited, and even hard, it may have been the effect of supernatural charity! » Such charity it must have been, allow me to believe, that did not hinder Don Orione from declaring to the Bishop who had disbanded his budding Congregation: « I think, my Lord, you may not in conscience celebrate Mass tomorrow. » Don Orione tells this himself; and a priest friend of his, writing in a religious periodical, comments on it referring to the *peccatum taciturnitatis* — the sin of silence — defined by theologians as « what Christians are guilty of in accustoming themselves to habitual indifference concerning the Church's problems. »

Not from today only, but today more clearly than before, we have been made aware of the presence of termites — secularist, Modernist, Marxist, Protestant — eating gaily away at the Church's framework — undermining, demolishing — under cover of the guardian's declared intention not to condemn anyone, or at least only to do so very

5

softly, keeping loud-voiced condemnation and scorn for such as we who deprecate prevailing fashion and sound the alarm; and this despite such deprecation being altogether in line with the Pope's Letter to the members of the first post-conciliar theological congress to meet in Rome in September 1966, strongly denouncing the « dangers of erroneous modern ideologies of such virulence as to threaten to subvert the very rational bases of the faith. »

Which brings me back to you and your March 7th 1965 — yours for what of yourself and your henchmen went into it — reformation day that marked the climax of a work declared by you, referring to « *the spirit and hopes that have led up to the Reform* », to have been under way in your diocese *for over ten years*. What a justification! — and one which, if accepted, justifies every abuse, and heresy: arbitrariness in matters of discipline, free inquiry in matters of worship, the making lawful of any and every sort of « experience » on the part of no matter whom and the setting up of a school — a mode — in the liturgical field, and in one church after another, whereby every priest is a pope in his own right, leaving the Pope nothing but to admonish and warn — state of affairs going far and away beyond that allowed even by your own dispositions themselves, already exceeding the Council's lawful ones. True enough your *way* of going to work has been quite the opposite of the hidden and silent one of the above-named insects.

No, it is hardly apt to speak of the termite as far as you are concerned, holding you as I do to be (except in intention, which was and is, assuredly, the opposite) the most formidable menace, after Martin Luther, to the Church's integrity and unity, first of her four marks: *one*, holy, Catholic and apostolic. Termites — popularly white ants —

eat away in the dark. Everything you have done has been proclaimed from the housetops and heralded by a blare of publicity. But there is one thing about your doings which has not been accorded such a blaze of light — I won't say it has exactly been kept dark — and that is the way you have managed to manoeuvre yourself into so useful and necessary a position as President of the *Consilium* for the carrying out of the conciliar Constitution on the Liturgy — Constitution good in itself, but in your hands distorted, violated, treated as a « scrap of paper ». Once arrived, and having yourself picked your auxiliaries, you never failed to act dictatorially, in the open, telecamera as often as not alongside. Indeed, this Wittemburg of yours — the launching of *your* reform — was preluded and accompanied by such a fanfare of propaganda as to be reminiscent of the inauguration of certain programmes of a bygone dictatorship régime. Poor St. Thomas, if in heaven it were possible for him to suffer on account of such an earthly turn of events!

That first Sunday of Lent, March 7th 1965, I blessed God, your Eminence, that a good dose of Russian fever (so the doctor called it, but let not your Lieutenants and orderlies take umbrage at that) spared me from church attendance and from being present, in that Catholic church of mine, at the first « divine service », at it was immediately called. It was surely only the effect of my fever, but do you know that day I fancied I heard, from the Lutherplatz in Worms, amid much mirthful cackling, a voice cry: « *At last! At last!...* »

THE TORN TUNIC

That first Sunday of Lent 1965 — *Laetare* Sunday for you — for me, as for so many others, a « Passion » Sunday — I was thinking of the Crucifixion, and I saw again in my mind the figure of Christ crucified in that painting the workman did not dare to strike with his pick-axe. I was thinking of the passage in the Gospel of St. John, to which the Church down the centuries has attributed, or rather recognised, such great symbolic value: « The soldiers therefore when they had crucified Him took His garments (and they made four parts, to every soldier a part) and also His tunic. Now the tunic was without seam, woven all of one piece. They said then one to another: let us not cut it, but let us cast lots whose it shall be, that the Scripture may be fulfilled, that says: They have parted my garments among them and for my tunic they have cast lots. » You may say it was the fever, your Eminence — or that the tunic, whether whole or in pieces, is always one tunic — but that Sunday I saw you, and so you have remained in my mind, in the act of doing to the seamless and blood-stained tunic of Christ what the soldiers did not dare to do, what none have ever dared to do, for all that such an act signifies: I saw you and I see you again *tearing to pieces that tunic which is the figure and bond of the unity of believers in Christ, past-present-and-future — tearing that tunic to shreds.*

Two years have gone by since the beginning of your « reform », during which time the fury for changing and smashing has become « sickening », verging on « iconoclastic », to use the pontiff's own words, already quoted. Again in His Apostolic Exhortation for the Year of Faith, *Petrum et Pau-*

lum Apostolos, proclaiming the 1967 celebrations in honour of the martyrdom in Rome of Sts. Peter and Paul, the Pope has spoken of « the attempt to introduce among God's people a so-called post-conciliar mentality that overlooks the firmness and coherence of the Council's ample and magnificent doctrinal and legislative developments... subverting the (Church's) spirit of traditional fidelity and spreading abroad the illusion of giving Christianity a new interpretation, one which is arbitrary and sterile... » Then, in His address to the members of the *Consilium* for the carrying out of the Constitution on the Liturgy, Paul VI at great length and with unprecedented severity castigated what He sumed up as a « *desacralization of the Liturgy — if still worthy of that name — and with it, fatally, of Christianity.* » Truly the Protestants themselves never accomplished quite so much as this in their four hundred years' history; and we, after only two years, are still rubbing our eyes, asking ourselves how it has been possible.

And for those that may object, *even against the Pope,* that to speak of iconoclasm is an exaggeration, as the liturgy was never meant to be an esthetic or artistic treasure and it was time it was « released from the fetters of emply ritual »; or those who, with the new theologians, have allowed themselves to be persuaded, mixing half-truths with truth, that though active liturgical worship was never intended merely to give a feeling of awe, being a « festive meal » celebrated in common, all the same, as at a banquet, a certain amount of adornment is becoming, here is what the Vatican *Osservatore Romano* had to say, but two months after the official introduction of your new way of community praying, on the shameful destruction of sacred art, a destruction constantly being carried out for all to see, altar candlesticks displayed as bargains in antique shops to be remodelled as dining-table lamps or curios for cocktail-bars, confessionals taken to pieces and made into bookcases and wardrobes, the altars themselves, with their marble and mosaic designs and friezes, recognisable in hotel reception rooms and the villas of the well-to-do, and even as bar-counters. « And that is not all », the article continues, « the priestly vestments which the alms of our ancestors, austere and sparing in their daily lives, had beautifully decorated for God's honour and worship, are cut up and refashioned into covers for divans and cushions... And still worse, the precious reliquaries now stand as ornaments between flower-vases and liqueur bottles... monstrances used to encase clocks and barometers. Even chalices are not spared from providing pedestals for lamps and profane statues in boudoirs on whose tables ashtrays made from patens show the sign of the cross when not covered with the ash of cigars... »

And this from Christopher Sykes, writing in *The Tablet*, less than a year later: « That the centuries which produced the greatest art in Europe made the liturgy accessible through accessible art is beyond question. Is that art inaccessible now? If so, then the liturgy on which it depends must be changed forthwith. But *is* it inaccessible? All the evidence is to the contrary, in the sense that the spread of education has spread an interest in such things, and that the clergy have only themselves to blame if they do not encourage this interest to the advantage of religion. The Philistines will always be with us, and at the moment they are « with it. » They are having a great time and their arguments are listened to. Few realise whither these arguments may tend. For if it is really considered that total « with-it-ness » is essential to a healthy Church, then it would seem that Chartres and all the cathedrals that descend from Chartres and all the great works of art that have adorned religion in succeeding centuries, should be made over to museums, and that the Church should go to other sorts of housing and use other means of expression in strict accordance with Pop art, and Pop ideas; and it will perhaps be hard after that to resist the Pop morality of our unlovely age. But suppose also that Sir Kenneth Clark's ideas (*) are not only true, but also seen to be so? What will new generations say of the men of the present time who seek to destroy their inheritance? Suppose men and women of the future get hold of old Missals and Holy Week books? What will they think of the men who threw them away? »

Yes, your Eminence, and we cannot help wondering what those will say of this March 7th of yours who live long enough to look back at this time as past history — not too long hence, please God, to prevent you yourself living to repent of your actions, and see them condemned, as did your precursor the Bishop of Pistoia. Those who live that long may see — but now I shall be laughed at for believing such a thing — that it was not for nothing the Devil was uncollared and unchained by doing away with the prayers which a great pope, Leo XIII, and another equally great, Pius XII, and yet another no less great, John XXIII, prescribed and prescribed again, jealously conserving them for the Church against the insidiously subverting assaults of Satan. Certain it is, in order to subvert, the best rule is to divide — *divide et impera!* — divide and rule — the exact opposite of the *Ut*

(*) That our age has diverted more of its genius into science than into art, and that while its science is sure to hold the respect of many ages to come, its art may be found to be ephemeral.

11

unum sint! — that they may be one; and to this, your Eminence, the present « reform » tends, to this it leads, howsoever different your intention.

That March 7th of yours marked the anti-Church's jubilee. And if it was only our fancy that made us hear the mocking laugh of Luther ring out from his monument in Worms — to which « dialogue » Catholics have lately been bringing flowers — it was in actual fact that we heard the rejoicing of Masons, as at an unimaginably great victory graciously granted them by their enemy the Church, to crown their prolonged struggles, conducted latterly in Parliament too, against a language which, for all its virtues, had but one defect in their eyes: that of being the language of the Church, of her unity, her Catholicity, her worship and her prayer.

History teaches what, from primeval times in this world, the unity of language has actually signified as regards the practical effects of union in any sense of the word. « And the earth was of one tongue, » Genesis says, « and of the same speech. » And there was peace. Discord came, and was called « Babel », « because there the language of all the earth was confounded ». And there was war. The Church, one in language in her universality, and one in her worship, was thereby always seen by the world's peoples — today more than ever weary of warring, more than ever hankering for union and peace — as the anti-Babel. The cementing unity possessed by her, aspired to by all, was always recognisable to all from her language. « *Ex omni gente magnum vinculum unitatis* »: marvellous bond of unity among all peoples. Pius XI, whose words these are, was only repeating after His predecessors what in turn was to be passed on to those that came after Him, one and all equally intent on keeping Latin for the Church, and through the

Church for the world. « The Church », again says Pius XI, « embracing all peoples and enduring until time shall have an end, by the very nature that is hers has need of a language that is UNIVERSAL, IMMUTABLE, NON-VERNACULAR... *sermonem suapte natura requirit universalem, immutabilem, non vulgarem...* Latin, so terse, so rich, so harmonious, so abounding in majesty and dignity we... can with good reason truly call *Catholic*: *dicere catholicam vere possumus* — words which another pope made his own, adding these further ones: « ...admirable bond by which the present age of the Church is bound to past and future: *vinculum peridoneum, quo praesens Ecclesiae aetas cum superioribus cumque futuris mirifice continetur.* »

Providential language, therefore — *language of God*, one might even say, as others indeed have: « *lingua qua locutus est Deus* » — providential in the finest sense of the word. Pius XI himself confirms this expressly, calling the language of Latium « admirably predestined — *mire comparatum* » — to serve the Church, herself predestined to have her centre in Rome, similarly willed centre of the Empire: *ad quem ipsa Imperii sedes tamquam hereditate pervenerit* — a thought of Dante's too well known to need further quotation here (*).

PREDESTINED LANGUAGE

It should not be for you, the archaeologists of ·Modernism, fanatics about « getting back to orig-

---

(*) « The Divine Comedy », *Hell*, II, 22-24.

ins » (as all spurious reformers) to wonder at this
going back of ours and to such high sources. For,
whether you like it or not, the truth is that Latin has
all the marks of being the predestined Catholic language. With Latin, prophetically, Virgil made the
Sibyl say: « Behold God! » — *Ait: Deus! Ecce Deus*
(Aeneid VI.46) thus and thereby announcing
His coming: « *Iam nova progenies coelo demittitur
alto* ». Horace, too, whose Odes heralded not a few
of the truths revealed by the Gospel not long after,
foretold, in his *Carmen Saeculare*, the future and
everlasting greatness of Rome and Latium. Latin
alone in Jerusalem, amid the Jewish shouts and
accusations, proclaimed and defended Him, through
the mouth of an innocent Roman woman, Claudia
Procla, wife of Pilate: « *Nihil tibi et iusto illi...* »
and that of Pilate himself, *judex iniustus*: « Why,
what evil has he done? »... *Quid enim mali fecit
iste? Nullam causam mortis invenio in eo...* » And
had it not been a Roman centurion first to utter
the Catholic Communion formula: *Domine, non
sum dignus...* again a Roman centurion who, on
Calvary, proclaimed Christ's divinity before the
Body of the Crucified: « *Vere filius Dei erat iste!* —
truly this man was the Son of God!... »
　　The Church — who in the Sacrament of the
Blessed Eucharist perpetually renews, but without
bloodshed, the Saviour's supreme Sacrifice, whose
mission is to propagate what was proclaimed by
the Roman soldier to the ends of the earth — made
the Latin language her own, the sign and instrument of her unity, the unity for which Christ
prayed, on his last evening on earth: « *Ut omnes
unum sint* — that they all may be one. » The
Church made Latin her own, upheld and defended
it all the more carefully and jealously the more her
children, multiplying and spreading over the face
of the earth, universalizing themselves in space and

14

time, were liable, without that bond, to become strangers from her, and among themselves. The Church preserved and guarded Latin, *made it loved*. She endowed it with highest poetry and greatest music, above all in what, of her very nature, is most essential and binding: prayer — the prayer of the liturgy — mindful of the Apostle's warning that it is not enough for God to be honoured « with one heart » unless also « with one mouth » — *ut unanimes, uno ore, honorificetis Deum*; and so the Church, image of the heavenly Court, has always chanted the eternal praises with one voice — *una voce* — *quam laudant Angeli atque Archangeli, Cherubim quoque ac Seraphim: qui non cessant clamare quotidie, una voce dicentes,* as the marvellous Preface of Trinity Sunday proclaims.

The notion of a universal language, Latin, of the universal Church, was extolled by a great lay champion of the Church's unity, worthy to rank with Dante in this, De Maistre (*), who wrote: « From pole to pole a Catholic enters the Church of his rite and is at home there, one of a family; and nothing is foreign to mind or heart. He hears there what from childhood he has heard and is able to join in the prayer and song of others around him, at once understanding and understood... » From the historical and philosophical standpoint De Maistre then adds: « The brotherhood resulting from a common language is a mysterious bond of untold power. In the ninth century Pope John VIII over-indulgently allowed the Slavs their own tongue in the celebration of the liturgy. But on reading a later Letter of the Pontiff's, the 95th, one hardly wonders at his admission of the drawbacks of such a dispensation. In fact, Gregory VII revoked it — but too late —too late to save the Rusisans — with

---

(*) Joseph De Maistre « *Du Pape* ».

what ultimate results only became evident in the course of time: Russia's separation from Rome, and the people's falling under the sway of a succession of « popes » all of whom, Stalin included, succeeded in being at the same time heads of State and heads of Church, despotically ruling Godless multitudes. »

The lengths to which minority language groups will go to guard their speech in respect to that of the country they are living in is proof, in the civil order, of what a tie of unity and devotion to the motherland a common language is. Italians have reason to know this among their frontier peoples. So is it, in the religious order, for the people of various lands in respect to their spiritual motherland, Holy Church. *Schisms and heresies have always been against Latin* — always pro vernacular, nationalistic — except insofar as Latin has at the same time been envied, for the evident barrenness of the branches cut off from the Vine compared with those that remained joined. National languages, national liturgies, are but the first step towards national churches, admitted, favoured, fostered and desired, with enticements and threats alternately, by the universal Church's avowed enemies — red, yellow or any other colour — well aware what division and destruction is thereby spelled for her, who is all of a oneness. Present historical situations are but repeating recent and ancient ones: Cardinal Mindszenty would not have been held, nor Cardinal Beran exiled, nor Cardinal Wyszinski obstructed, and so many others, their brethren and ours, would not be impeded or in prison but free, honoured and salaried *had their Catholicism not spoken Latin*. This is tantamount to saying that, if the Church could have various centres and heads in Budapest, Prague, Warsaw, Moscow and Pekin, instead of one in

Rome, things would have happened and be happening differently. Has it not made you reflect a little, your Eminence, that your brother prince of the Roman Church, Poland's Primate — in whose land, as everyone knows, the government is exerting all possible pressure to nationalise (in other words annihilate) Christ's Church — together with the Episcopate has turned down your March 7th « reform », allowing no more than the Epistle and Gospel to be read in Polish?

INNOVATION, AND A MATTER OF FEELING

To give God worthiest honour, the Church, the divine Spouse, in this predestined language — of all, because in particular of none — language perennially evergreen as the olive — composed words with music of the greatest beauty and fittingness for the celebration of her liturgy so that, with one voice in all the sacred buildings of the world, the Psalmist's cry should be heard: « How beautiful are Thy Tabernacles, O Lord! » — and that those who might enter as strangers should stay, as brethren with others, to worship and adore.

You, your Eminence, certainly cannot be unaware how it was that many in the past found their way to the Church *through the Church*, in Dante's phrase « following the Bridegroom for love of the Bride, His Church », seen and heard on earth in her holy and moving rites and ceremonies, in all their supernatural, outward beauty. But, on the other hand, it should also not be unknown to you how today, after your « reform », not only in certain countries has the stream of conversions showed signs of drying up but many Catholics themselves stand aloof, no longer at home — if they have not gone away altogether, estranged and desolate, making their own the lament of Jeremiah: « How solitary is the City now... her friends have despised her and become her enemies... her adversaries have become her Lords, her enemies are enriched... and from the Daughter of Sion all beauty has vanished. » And: « Is this the City of perfect beauty, the joy of all the earth?... How dim the gold has become, the finest colours are changed: the stones of the Sanctuary are scattered... » Sorrowful plaint, your Eminence, which there is no need to turn into the New Testament first Good Friday cry: « *Quid feci tibi* — O, my people, what have I done to you? » The answer you yourself had already made (telecamera, as always, alongside) in a press conference three days before the memorable and historic March 7th 1965. At that conference, I counted the number of times you used the word « reform » (ugly and typically Protestant word), with the same delight as the word love could be heard on the lips of one betrothed: forty times. As adamant as you have shown yourself to us, so we to you, not without letting you know, however, that in this hardness of yours is recognised sincere zeal (which it is our wish to return). Also, in this hardness, humility is recognised, your wish to be all things to all, little with the little, of the people with the people — though, to our way of thinking, in a way somewhat out of keeping with the dignity of your office — such as to appear plain softness in the eyes of some.

And the impression given by your priests, who appear so fond of disporting themselves and joking before the telecameras, is that, instead of these being a necessary nuisance, a trial to be put up with for their utility, they are a kind of hobby to be passionately indulged. Nor, I confess, and it may seem spiteful, on another televised occasion did your Eminence's sense of personal decorum and seemliness strike one as any too apparent, viewing that televised image of yours jocularly intent on hurling streamers and scattering confetti in the Carnival, with a gusto and a dash to justify you a permanency in episcopal service despite the new seventy-five-year limit (*ad multos annos*, your Eminence, if you will allow me, in Latin). Indeed, you acted with a shade *too much* élan if, as was reported in the papers, whilst joining in these pre-Lenten Carnival frolics, you actually lost your ring in the heat of the moment — unless, of course, it was your intention to carry the Gospel injunction « *Unless you become as little children...* » to the extent of indulging in street games, in this case a kind of Bo-Peep, not with sheep gone astray, but a shepherd.

Nor, in our opinion (but *that* need not mean it seemed so to others) did it appear any more in keeping with the dignity of your Purple your appearing in a spacious beauty parlour — need one say, on television — unctuous and smiling, at that ladies' hair- dressing competition, the cardinal-atial robes creating an undeniably striking effect amid the frantically flashing combs and billowing tresses. I would here just like to recall (but *my* opinion only, naturally) in what a different style this « going out to meet the people » — phrase on everybody's lips now — can be accomplished, and how, indeed, it has been done in the past, for example by another prince of the Church, the for-

mer Archbishop of Florence Cardinal Dalla Costa.
From such Carnival scenes as these, anyway,
it can more easily be understood how it is that you
have been able yourself, without the slightest comp-
unction, to throw to the pigs those pearls — patrimony of faith, poetry and piety — committed to
your care — patrimony which, if you did not respect, you might at least have judged worth respecting
from the universal veneration and admiration accorded it by others for fifteen centuries. *Quae
ignorant blasphemant* — people insult what they
do not understand — a matter of *taste*, then, let
it be said, excusing you and your collaborators in
their work of hewing and hacking down all that is
« old and non-functional ».

The excuse you graciously found in *our* regard,
as to our objections, was condescendingly uttered
by you at yet another press conference of yours,
with that never-failing smilingness: something you
grant us as having, but you glory only in not having — sentiment, *feeling*. « Yours is a *sentimental*
standpoint, » you declared, « a sentimental standpoint obviously seeking non-sentimental justification. » (I gave up trying to count the number of
times the word sentiment recurred in your conference.) And without going to the lengths of calling
us foolish and silly people, you attributed this
standpoint of ours to *age* — a matter of *years* —
weakness on the part of some elderly priests and
others having got past, shall we say, their golden
jubilee. « Even among the clergy » (to quote your
conference) « there is naturally some difficulty in
certain quarters, especially among those of somewhat advanced years, in easily welcoming this
reform, in breaking the habits of half a century
daily maintained.. » And to the amiable interpo-
lation of the TV moderator, implying you yourself
were no chicken, not exactly in your prime, but

were an innovator, you gave an airy affirmative.
« Yes, that is right: I am an innovator — I already
was — I already felt these things, so it doesn't cost
me anything to carry them out now. » To be sure,
it does not cost you anything — *you were already
carrying out « these things »*, as you have told us
(not only feeling them) referring to the reforming
« experiment » in Rome's Borromini Hall which —
in the spirit of anticipation which led you to dero-
gate from the law in force — was to see and hear
the first yé-yé Mass, little more than a stone's throw
from St. Peter's.

That these things do not cost you anything one
can well believe, for you are indeed coherent, no
sentimentalist, you. But the fact that there were
priests who actually died of heartbreak (as is known
to you) at being brusquely, brutally and unreason-
nably obliged once and for all to abandon the Mass
they were bound to more than anything in the
world by a life-time's most sacred and dear ties —
that there were others, as you also are aware, who
on that morning of March 7th 1965 had tears in
their eyes as they forced themselves to pronounce
the opening words of the new rite — yours — by
which was perverted, at the foot of an altar turned
the wrong way round, a tradition as « ancient but
ever-new as the village fountain » (Pope John's
words) — all that is « sentiment » to you; and sentiment, feeling, it is indeed, but not sentimentalism,
the connotation you give the word.

Yes, that feeling, sentiment, was never found
in your make-up, your Eminence, that it is a complex you are not guilty of, one must suppose,
wondering if even your first Mass, that far off
morning of 1914, holds no memories that move you.
One must suppose that already the Latin irked you,
that grudgingly and without conviction you went
through all the reverential acts the rubrics bade

you perform. Recently, by this second Instruction that came into force on June 29th, Feast of Sts. Peter and Paul, you have got rid of still more of these « anachronistic and superfluous gestures » (according to the progressive and « liberal » press) — gestures and reverences too servile — even in respect to the Presence of Christ — for the President of the new democratic assembly of the People of God. How it must have pained you to have to bend your knee in the middle of the Crede at the *Incarnatus est*, which in us poor sentimental folk always induced feelings — yes, flesh-and-blood *feelings* of reverence and love. And how it must have offended your ears to hear the Sanctus bell thrice rung (there are present-day disciples of yours, members of the clergy, who forbid servers to ring the bell *under pain of mortal sin*). This festal acclamation, joined by chimes from the belfry, used in many country parts of Italy to be prolonged until the moment of His coming down upon the altar, so that all within hearing, also without in field and farmstead, could know and unite in prayer.

Now, seeing the abuses, indiscipline and disorder unleashed by that first Instruction of yours, we may be allowed to wonder what, before long, in practice, will be the outcome of this second, once again in the direction of adaptation to modern society and the world, national custom, and « desacralization », still more reducing the margin between the sacred and the profane (*). Genuflect-

---

(*) The answer your Eminence himself has already supplied in the warning sent out by you (21.VIII.67), to all national episcopal conferences and liturgical commissions, that private and arbitrary experiments « are gravely threatening the future of the whole liturgical reform », in a situation now « a great deal more alarming than two years ago... » — situation summed up by the parish priest who confused the close of a new-rite nuptial service by saying: « Go to Mass — the peace is finished! »

ions, bending and kissing the relic of the altar, above all the making of the sign of the Cross, anachronistic and superfluous gestures! Speed, brevity, convenience, democratization are taken account of; but why only the less positive aspects of modernity, which is far from being devoid of mystical sense and appreciation of beauty? Why not, then, a move in the direction *of increased* solemnity — *secundum naturam ipsius actionis sacrae* — of *added* awe and loveliness? Nor is democracy the only form of government, which can well give way to another. And then what further new adjustments to the world and the times might be deemed necessary? In the Principality of Monaco, Montecarlo, your Eminence may be aware, Masses are still said, as ever, *versus Tabernaculum*, and in the Church's traditional and supernational language.

As for the « liberty » and « elasticity » of the *Instructio altera* of June 29th, extolled in a note of explanation published in the *Osservatore Romano* by Fr Bugnini for allowing choice of certain gestures and signs the celebrant may make or may omit (though bound to omit others) it was evident enough from his second and lengthy explanation how far from satisfied many Bishops and clergy in actual fact were with the vaunted « flexibility of application ». This was deliberate, Fr Bugnini explained, and if « dutifully taken advantage of, most useful lest authority be imposed regarding this or that norm of no fundamental importance. » All in the name of modernity and democracy — but anarchy is the outcome; and why, it may be pertinently asked, if norms have no fundamental importance, must people be burdened with them? This « flexibility of application », we were further asked to believe by Fr Bugnini, is also « an education in principles of adaptation ». One has heard it called

something else by members of the clergy: *education in encouraging a different rite in every parish.*
A vital aspect of the Church's visible unity is effectively hit. It has, also, been partly because of the same sacred signs and gestures, universally repeated by the priest at the altar, that the Mass of the Latin rite has always been understood and followed by the people in any place, whether their knowledge of Latin was small or great. The liturgy, as Paul VI's encyclical *Mysterium fidei* does but reaffirm, « occupies first place in the Church's life. » It is only logical that, if there is liturgical disruption and disunity, this is the chief threat to the Church's internal order and peace.

We are sometimes told, these days, by your followers, your Eminence, and many now unthinkingly repeat it, that we must sacrifice our personal feelings in these matters for the greater good of the greater number of tomorow's Church. This will help us to accustom ourselves and accept unwelcome and repulsive changes and innovations, suddenly introduced. Apart from the fact that it is the Church of *today* we live in, and that if *this* is right the future will probably be able to take care of itself, did you ever hear the old-fashioned country proverb that says: « A cat in too much of a hurry has blind kittens »?

THE « DIAPHRAGM »

It is told of Bl. Dominic Bàrberi, Apostle of England, that he applied himself with such loving zest as a young student to his Latin studies that in a short time, helped by a prodigious memory, and the Holy Spirit, he was able to repeat a whole page by heart after a single reading. Similar feats

are recounted of Pius XII. But God knows, your
Eminence, for how long Latin must have been
irking you. Your learning would seem to exclude
this dating from school days, as in my case, and
ill-taught, boring Latin exercises. For, not satisfied
with giving vent to your feelings, and with taking
consequent action, you went so far as to let slip
in regard to her language certain words against
the Church which greater reflection would have
safely left to her enemies, Masons, Marxists and
Protestants, even if they were uttered in « dialogue »
frame of mind — dialogue which, with you and
yours, amounts to nothing but a sort of penitential,
self-accusing monologue — a continual *confiteor-
peccavi-mea culpa-miserere* recited in sackcloth and
ashes at their feet, with offers of love and repara-
tion which do but end, as all excesses, in nausea-
ting and driving the « separated brethren » still
farther from us — to say nothing of those die-hard
champions of 20th century British Protestantism
reported in the press as having advised their supporters to have no more dealings now whatever
with the Church of Rome as she is clearly hand in
glove with Communism, judging from the published and priest-backed efforts of the Catholic
Marxists.

To say, as you have repeatedly done in public (and not once only) that Latin is a « dividing line » — a « diaphragm » — between the priest
presiding over the assembly and the assembled; to
speak outright, as again you have, of « caste » in
church, which your reform set out to obviate by
« removing every dividing line » making for distinctions between a privileged, lettered class and an
unlettered, unprivileged one of averagely educated
people understanding only the comon language, is
properly to plagiarize the language of the Church's
opponents, not to say their way of thinking. It is

to represent the Church until now, until your time, as the enemy of the poor, and of the mass of people, the friend of the well-to-do, and upper classes. It is to infer (putting the best light possible upon it) that, until you came, the Church had been misguided, not on the right track, not really understanding anything and therefore doing nothing, by her liturgy, to bring souls to God. Yet the Church, even ordinary, everyday men and women may be dimly aware, had persons of intelligence before you, the Church growing and spreading in the world before March 7th 1965. The Church in the last fifteen hundred years and more has even had some holy people — saints — servants of the poor, loved by the people, spending themselves wholly in their service, for love of God, and to the point of martyrdom: unlettered saints as St. Isidore, men of letters like St. Thomas Aquinas. But one and all, saints and people, drew from the Latin liturgy and Mass the wisdom and humility, charity and piety and spirit of sacrifice which so greatly raised them up and strengthened them. You, your Eminence, cannot possibly be unaware, so that it would be impertinent of me to try and excuse you on the grounds of ignorance, of what the Church has done in the past (without having to call herself, as now, « the Church of the poor » — there was no need) against what you call « caste », for the good of the people — things in regard to which your friends the Catholic progressives are base, vacuous, verbose demagogues, not the *avant-garde* at all but towed along at the tail of others who, in matters of demagogy, are past masters, fomenting and making use of your own ecclesiastical demagogy only to boost their own, pulling faces at you behind your back the while. Not a bit backward they over inviting you to give them a hand — as indeed a well-known Marxist leader actually did — in ridding the world of true religion! None of your « true and authentic people » as you call them, ever dreamed of thinking themselves an underprivileged, discriminated against « caste » in church, until you gave them the idea. None of the people — true and authentic or otherwise — ever asked for this « reform ». Nor can it be called « democratic », exactly, the way you foisted it upon them, in the name of the democratic Church, without so much as consulting a single parish priest, head of Catholic organisation or member of the laity. The truth is that the average person before never felt himself in the very least divided from any privileged class, any more than others better off, or betted educated, ever felt themselves cut off from the average, all being one with the priest at the altar and on the highest spiritual level, to which they were incited to rise according to personal, individual capacity. Now, one and all find themselves forced, willy-nilly, and with no means of escape, down to the same lowest level: the communal but chaotic and disjointed, regimented but distractingly ragged and disorderly babble of a vernacular service so ignoble, so banal beyond belief, and at the same time so *obscure* also as to extort from one of your own lieutenants, Fr Balducci, the word « barbarous », and make another, no less yours, dub « intolerably ugly and altogether inadmissable in prayerful language ». As to the boasted intelligibility of the vernacular and the new liturgy of the word, this is here and there so transparent as to require of the more obliging members of the clergy the not infrequent and grotesque service of re-translation into the actual everyday language. « With this new-fangled Mass and way of doing things one can't make head or tail of it », a good woman was heard to declare, speaking for many

who, out of respect for the clergy, are often reluctant to speak frankly — remark which, if at all
representative, could qualify some of our vernacular texts as matter for the former Holy Office
Index for betraying the spirit of divine worship —
« *qui cultui divino detrahunt* ».

When all is said and done, even if things were
not as I have shown them to be, the very *untranslat-
ability* of the Latin sacred texts, as proved by the
monstrous renderings, has resulted in a sorry state
of affairs and it remains true that *you*, by putting
up this barrier — this « diaphragm » *between the
people and Latin* — have humiliated them — and
in what manner: hopelessly uneducated, you have
thereby labelled them (for you, evidently, they can
learn nothing on the score of its being never too
late to mend, although one might have thought it
were too late to mend the presumed harm done by
centuries of Latin) — and so, as uneducated *igno-
rami* you leave them and deal with them. But that
need not worry anyone: as you have dealt with
them, so you deal with all — all are to be equals
in ignorance.   Could popularism be more abject
and idiotic? — imitation, in the religious sphere,
of the worst, most outmoded, regressive, doctrin-
aire, stick-in-the-mud Marxism.

BOTTOM-RUNG EQUALITY

Time was when Communism, of the Roman
brand, used to be dinning it into the heads of the
proletariate: « One day you shall also eat the best
food, be well-dressed, have your own car, travel
first class, see what shows you like and send your

children to high-class schools », only adding : « And we shall make the upper classes eat bread and cheese, go to work in factories and field, on foot or by tram, and hold their heads down; and woe betide any that try and raise them! » A Communism made of hate for a particular class, in whose position it wants to be, rather than love for the people — a hate that is still a driving force, but now serving to turn the wheels of a more modern and attractive party programme. Those that once were wont to claim « the land for the workers », have now taken to saying : « The land for the gentry — if they like to work it » — they, the workers, preferring to occupy high-class flats complete with labour-saving gadgets, and imitation antique furniture. They, the working people, now require to eat, sleep, travel, pursue sport and be entertained *like gentlemen* — all on a higher level, the cultural included. *Non in solo pane vivit homo* — man does not live by bread alone; and they, the « true and authentic people » have understood it, if only partly, showing themselves in many branches of learning eager and willing scholars.

You, though, with your « people's liturgy », not to say « class liturgy » — your dunce treatment of them, have only succeeded in dragging into church and into the Church's prayer and worship just such a hopelessly and offensively outmoded mentality as marked the tactics of that earlier Communism, making it even more vulgar by the shamefully concocted texts thrust upon us : « The Mass of the asses », one has heard the new rite called — by the people.

These asses, then, ignorant of Latin through no past fault of theirs, you and your school are not now going to make the mistake of instructing in what they do not understand. Donkeys eat straw and with straw you will provide them, imposing, what is more, on all alike the same provender. No longer, then, *In nomine Patris, et Filii, et Spiritus Sancti*, which Italians cannot possibly be expected to understand means, in their own language, *In nome del Padre e del Figliolo e dello Spirito Santo*, nor *Confiteor Deo omnipotenti*, but *Confesso a Dio onnipotente;* and as for *Gloria* actually meaning *gloria*, *Credo credo*, and so many other words and phrases almost identical... But there is no use in enlarging upon this. Let readers of other European Latin nations — and also non-Latin — divert themselves by thinking of similar comparisons, a good deal fewer, of course, than with Italian. Even with Japanese, a learned Jesuit, once a missionary, has remarked, mere children can in a very short time be got to understand the essentials, let alone adults, *if they want to, and the effort is made with them.* As Evelyn Waugh wrote not long before he died in a letter to *The Tablet*, « Certainly many cannot follow the Latin liturgy any more than an infant can understand the words that are spoken at its Baptism. But the flow of grace is not impeded by vocabulary », as those evidently think who are more intent on having us raise our voices, than our minds and hearts — in which case, the flow of grace can be disastrously impeded.

I conclude this chapter by quoting at length another letter of the great English Catholic writer, published not long before the zero hour of your « reform »: « I do not believe that complete verbal comprehension is necessary for prayer. Most of the liturgies of the historic religions, Christian and heathen, have been incomprehensible to most of the faithful. Lately... there has been a prophetess of Zambia who stirred up a whole province to ferocious ecstasies by playing records (in English, of which the people knew nothing) of Sir Winston Churchill's speeches... I am not, of course, advocating such extreme measures. But in the traditional Mass it was easy to know by a glance at the priest's movements the precise place he had arrived at. The « participation » so much now spoken about did not require any special grace of prayer. It was simply the exaltation of the soul silently to cooperate in what was being done at the altar... The curse of Babel is more divisive than colour or class or nationality... Like any other destructive movement, if successful, this will be irremediable. There will be no restoration of Latin once the tradition is broken, however much our descendents come to deplore the loss ».

SCANDAL IN CHURCH

This story is still told in Tuscany of a farmer who took his baby son to be baptised in the times of the Grand Duke Leopold: so blissfully happy was he, along with relatives and friends — it happened also to be Eastertide — that no attention was paid by any at first to the lame and halting words the celebrant, obliged to use the vernacular, was murmuring aloud in place of the accustomed splendid Latin prayers. But all things come to an end and suddenly, at a certain point in the rite, the farmer pricked up his ears and shook himself, hardly able to believe what he had heard: instead of the triple invocation *per Deum vivum, per Deum verum, per Deum sanctum*, as his hand traced the sign of the Cross upon the infant's forehead the priest was

exclaiming what soundel like: « By the living God!
... ...by God!... ...holy God! »... Before the last words
were out of his mouth, casting a quick look around
to make sure he was not dreaming, and certain he
was not from the astonished eyes of the others,
especially his better half standing by with the baby
in her arms, the good man jumped forward with:
« Quick, Eliza, take the child out of here and let's
be off with us! — *priest's swearing* ».

A Prelate of the Roman Curia has left on record
an anecdote of his first experience of saying Mass
in the vernacular: « The first time I did so was
with some reluctance in the hope of pleasing a
group of seminarians. It was Lent 1965 and the
Holy Mass I had to celebrate started with the prayer: « Save us, O Lord, from the horns of buffa-
loes and the teeth of lions!... » I could not help
pausing, in some embarrassment, for I perceived
the young men around me — who had arrived, as I,
at the church in a whirl of cars and buses, without
catching sight of a single lion or buffalo — were
looking at me with bulging eyes, and some were
suppressing laughter. I thought then, and I think
now, that the use of the everyday language in the
celebration of Mass does not, on all occasions, solve
the problem of making the Holy Sacrifice more
understandable to the people. Better — much
better — understand little, than understand ill. »

Compelled to realise this yourself, and to do
something about it so as to avoid giving occasion
for stares, laughter and scandal there never was
with Latin, you resorted to yet another remedy
worse than the evil (of your making) which you
had to seek to cure. Instead of admitting that
things could well have been left as they were, rather than admit failure of any kind, you determined on expurgation of the Missal here and there,

making it something *ad usum delphini*... Paying no
regard to Pope Pius XII who, in *Mediator Dei*,
condemned and accused of « rash audacity » any
who dared cut out « from the lawful books of public prayer sacred writings of the Old Testament
on the grounds that these are little suited to our
times », you emasculated the Missal, taking from
it, « for reasons of morality », the story of the
chaste Susanna who, given the choice by the two
elders, in their lust for her great beauty, of sinning
with them or having them bear false witness against
her that would mean death, immediately chose
death. Saved from this fate by the providential
judgement of the boy Daniel, faithful to her husband and to God in heroic manner, Susanna came
to typify the Church herself, tempted, persecuted
yet triumphing, in whose catacombs and churches
she is portrayed, one of Rome's ancient Lenten
Stations being dedicated to her. In the Mass of
this fourth Sunday of Lent, the Epistle taken from
the 13th chapter of Daniel relates her trial, and the
blessedness of her proven innocence, prefiguring
the Gospel narrative of the woman taken in adult-
ery, pardoned by Jesus with the warning: « Go and
sin no more. » Now, this Mass as you have made
it is lopsided, only the New Testament adulteress
remaining. The blameless Susanna, freed by Daniel from unjust stoning, you have now stoned, pro-
nouncing it imprudent to read aloud before the
Christian people, of high, average or little education, the vernacular equivalent of what for centuries had been read by the priest in Latin, and followed in the bilingual missals of the world by all
who would: « *Exarserunt in concupiscentia eius...* »
« *contemplantes eam...* » « *nos in concupiscentia
tui sumus...* » « *assentire nobis et commiscere no-
biscum...* » « *concubuit cum ea...* » and so on. With

Latin, it must be allowed, certain problems never existed. They understood who were able to understand. The « candle », to which Paul VI has likened Latin prayer and Plainsong in the Divine Office, stood upon the bushel, as did the old household lamp, shedding light without glare — bringing to mind that verse of the immortal English Jesuit, Gerard Manley Hopkins, on the Most Blessed Virgin « compared to the air we breathe »:

> *... Through her we may see Him*
> *Made sweeter, not made dim,*
> *And her hand leaves His light*
> *Sifted to suit our sight.*

LATIN AND THE PEOPLE

« Latin is dead and done with! » a vernacular enthusiast was heard crowing on the steps of the church after the first triumph that Sunday morning of March 7th, adding — for the Catholic habit of years and centuries dies hard — « *Deo gratias!* » Then, seeing he had made others coming out from « divine service » laugh a little, thought to make them laugh a bit more, continuing: « Yes, done with at last, for good and all, *laus Deo, per omnia saecula saeculorum!* And, if you like it better that way, then *prosit!* As for me, I say: *Requiescat in pace!* »

One is reluctant to believe this good man's prognostication is well founded. As a matter of fact, true findings as opposed to trumped up figures show the number of Latin supporters and lovers of the Roman liturgy to be far greater than imagined, and steadily growing. This despite what the public are led to believe in the Catholic papers, or by polls whose statistical results are either false or not really representative, for various reasons — apart from the fact that, even if they were, the majority saying they like something does not necessarily make it right for them, democratic Church or no. What is right and best for people must always, in the long run, be only what is objectively good and true. Anyway, there are reasons for hoping that the future of the Church's Latinity, and also of another Latin, scholastic, may be bright, from the interest, paradoxically enough, of the working people — at any rate, in Italy — with their natural intelligence and good sense, their native flair for what is sound and beautiful — hope from the best sons of the people turned scholar, for whom your demagogy and donkey treatment has little to offer but universal bottom-rung equality. Interesting to note, too, in this respect, that when two or three years ago Italy's first squinter government (one eye to the Left, the other to the Right) began bowing to the Masonic-Marxist brotherhood, humiliating the populace by making Latin facultative in the schools instead of compulsory, those freely opting for Latin turned out to be the very children of the proletariate whose good had been made the pretext for abolishing the subject — move in reality engineered out of hatred for the Church as a first step on the way to others. *Out of hatred for the Church*, it cannot be emphasized too clearly, *and for the Church's universal, supernational language.* A declaration of the Undersecretary of the Italian Ministry of Education recently said that a majority of secondary school pupils had opted for Latin as facultative subject in the last three years, the greater part of these from outlying districts and suburbs, which means that those most « of the people » deliberately made choice of Latin and a Latin a good deal more difficult than the liturgical. The Undersecretary, not himself a master of language, added: « without there being any discrimination of a social character » (what he *meant* to say was irrespective of class distinctions) showing that, contrary to what you maintain, your Eminence, Latin tends not to create or even encourage « caste », but to lessen and eliminate it.

If the Italian public authorities had been in less of a hurry (unlike the proverbial cat) they would have taken into account the late phenomenon in Communist-ruled countries, beginning with Czechoslovakia, of Latin's being reinstated — « in the name of the people » and of « the people's education and the raising of their standards » — as a compulsory subject in every school, putting us Italians and Catholics to shame. And now that these iron-curtain lands have in this way given the all-clear there is, perhaps, some hope of one day seeing Latin — scholastic and liturgical — return to favour.

So much for the Church's political and ideological opponents. Now, what about her other time-honoured theological and religious antagonists? One heard of that article in *The Times* not so long ago reporting paradoxically that, whilst the Council in Rome was making it a question whether to substitute the vernacular speech of each country for Latin in the Catholic Church's worship, Anglicans, on the other hand, after four hundred years' experience of the vernacular, were in some quarters making endeavours to introduce Latin into divine service, sincerely deploring their lack, which puts them in the position, not unlike that of the envious and incredulous proletariate and Communists, of having plenty of sacks, but no flour, amazed to see those that have flinging it away, like handfuls of confetti into the gutter during the empty-headed frivolities of a Carnival.

It is of course well known that among those most sincerely desirous of recovering lost Christian unity there is a movement (sanctioned by the Synod of Canterbury) for a return to Latin, language in which all once prayed in union with Rome before separation from the centre and seat of unity, and the abandoning in this way of their Father's House. « Have no illusions », Bruce Marshall wrote recently. « It will not be any liturgy celebrated in the common language that will succeed in making those invited come to the marriage festivities. The Anglican church continues to pray and chant in the most elegant English before the emptiest of pews; whilst the least knowledgeable Catholic more of less ignorant of Latin understands perfectly what is being done by the monks of Solesmes. » (*) And in a book he published called *Rome and Reunion* the American Episcopalian Observer-Delegate at the Council, Professor Frederick Grant, makes an impassioned plea for the oldest part of the Roman Mass, which, he says, can easily be learned, *but cannot be satisfactorily translated out of Latin into any other language.*

(*) An Anglican scholar, Fr Gregory Dix, has recalled how Our Lord, Who chose to found His Church in Roman-occupied Palestine, « never attended a vernacular service in His life. Alike in Temple and synagogue, the services were in the liturgical Hebrew which was not understood by the people without special instruction » — reminder to be reflected on by vernacularists liking to remind us that Our Lord spoke Aramaic. Nor, for that matter, were either early Christian liturgical Greek or the Latin that succeeded it the currently spoken language, they were sacral forms of it.

THE TORN TUNIC

It is a matter for wonder and admiration, but really quite logical and coherent, that foremost and fiercest of the defenders of the Latin liturgy should be the English-speaking peoples, the Americans and other non-Latin Northerners such as the Germans, the Poles, the Swiss, the Scandinavians — peoples either predominantly Protestant, or ethnically and linguistically most different from Rome, who might have been thought to have greater reason to countenance, if not positively welcome *en bloc*, your vernacular « reform » than the Italians for whom Latin, Dante said, is « our own tongue. »

The widespread loss of love for the Latin liturgy has been felt with particular acuteness in these lands by converts, who formerly experienced all the disadvantages of divine service in the ordinary language, an experience from which, in coming to the universal Church of Rome, they believed themselves to have been freed forever. The Latin liturgy is impersonal. Through the priest celebrating at the altar, those following are enabled to unite with his Sacrifice, in mind and heart, without having to be involved in his personality, or even being aware of it. With the vernacular Mass, the priest's personality — intruding still more when celebrating *versus populum* — cannot escape becoming prominent and a distraction, when it is not a real hindrance, to divine worship and a spiritual taking part. « It is sad », the English Latin Mass Society (extended to Australia and America) noted in one of their early Bulletins, « that it has required such an upheaval in the Church to discover what was always obvious to so many, particularly converts... »

English and German Catholics who know something of nationalistic liturgical reformation ruth-
lessly thrust on the people in the name of puri-
fication, getting back to origins, and even of the
Holy Spirit and truth, are aware if only from their
history books of the part played in the introduction and dissemination of heresy by the enforced
use of the common language in place of Latin.
English people in particular have on record what
was said by St. Thomas More: « First in many
places they sang the service in their mother tongue,
men and women and all, and that was a pretty
sport for them for awhile. But after a little use
thereof, the pleasure of the novelty passed, and
they set somewhat less thereby than a man's song.
They changed also the Mass, and soon after that
many cast it up clean. » (I know of some present-
day Italian families, formerly regular and devout
in their religious duties, who now say they prefer
to say their prayers at home rather than attend
what is more like « Sunday-school class » than the
Mass).

In a letter to the Bishops of England and Wales
this year the Latin Mass Society, whose President is the world-famed Catholic writer and apo-
logist, Sir Arnold Lunn, confirmed that in England
now children are being brought up to believe that
Latin is only a symbol of an outdated religion.
But there are many Catholic parents, cherishing
the beliefs and practices of the Church of their parents, or to which they became converted, who
are determined that their own children shall not
be denied the benefits of its glorious traditions.

And lastly, as regards England, here is what
the *Clergy Review* published last year, concluding a « Letter » signed by T. Charles-Edwards:
« For four centuries it (the Latin Mass) has, in the

minds of ordinary Englishmen, served to distinguish the Church of Rome from the crowd of conflicting Christianities as they stumbled and slithered towards their logical conclusion. Insofar as it disappears, Englishmen will conclude that the Church of Rome is no more than one of « the Churches », one of those increasingly unfamiliar organisations in which their grandmothers believed and their grandfathers would have liked to believe, and in which they themselves were baptized and married... Do not forget that phrase of Chesterton's: *Wickedly wearying of the best.* There is a power of percipience in that adverb. »

In America, the writings of the world-renowned philosopher Dietrich von Hildebrand have done much in resisting spurious reforms and the drift away from tradition. Confirmation of the deeply rooted traditional conviction of U.S. Catholics (despite what the *avantgarde* press and clergy are making out) was had from the enquiry conducted in 1966 by some *130 newspapers and magazines* as to the reception accorded your « reform » by Americans: a definite *not appreciated* was reported on the part of an overwhelming majority (mentioned with amazement by the Vatican's *Osservatore Romano*), reasons given being « a sense of weakening of religious practices, and also of spiritual ties with fellow Christians ». Converts from various forms of Protestantism said: « This new turn of the liturgy brings us back to the Church we once belonged to and takes away that characteristic Catholic devotion and piety that had such an influence upon our conversion. » From which once again may be seen clearly enough that the dividing line is not, and never was, the universal Roman liturgy, but nationalistic rites held in the vernacular. The United

States Catholic Traditionalist movement, too, has given ample testimony of this, and more.

Then in Canada, Professor John Buell aroused widespread admiration by his article published in *Unity*, Montreal: « ... the important point is the Mass *has been changed enough to pull it out of its former context*... Gone the magnificent organ and choral singing in centuries-sacred Latin, gone the sacral language in which *all* really important holiness-bestowing things were done and gone all the smaller acts of devotion (what will Prof. Buell be saying now, after your June 29th Instruction?) which stemmed from these. The tone, the style, *has been changed*... and the absoluteness of the sacred, the absolute sacredness we had projected into these things, that is gone. » And the conclusion: « The result has not been a new spirituality, a new psychology of faith and adoration. The result has been no spirituality, a confused faith and a problematical adoration... To ask people to change, without offering them a basis from which to change, is to test their belief, not in God, nor in His Church, whom they cannot fight, but in the experts, whom they can and will resist. »

Let me now quote in full a page from *Romanitas and the Present Catholic Moment* by the eminent German man of letters, Professor Anton Hilckmann, of Magonza University: « Until now, Latinity has been for us, at least as regards feeling and devotion, something really of the *essence* of the faith we profess. In a far greater way than is generally imagined in the linguistically Latin countries, Latin, the language of the liturgy, for us linguistically non-Latin Europeans (but religiously all the more Roman and thence Latin) was a *sacred* language. The very thought of its one day being touched would have seemed *sacrilege*. Certainly one loved and sang with enthusiasm religious hymns and songs in German... but the *liturgy* in its strictest sense, the *Mass*, for instance, in German — absolutely no: *that was inconceivable.* The times of the Protestant Reform were past history but not all that distant and people did not forget how their ancestors had had to take up arms against a whole series of Protestant princelings to keep the *Latin* Mass, to keep our faith's *Romanity*, to prevent our religion from becoming *Germanized* (« *Cuius regio, eius religio* »), something abhorred, an *abomination* never then, and never since, accepted by the Catholic conscience of our forbears. The Roman Mass in the Latin tongue was for us the most splendid and eloquent manifestation and demonstration of the *world unity of our faith*, which we looked on as the one true faith of all mankind... That was what Catholicism and Catholicity signified: *the whole world as our fatherland.* To be a Catholic meant, in a more than earthly sense, to be a citizen of the universe, of all the world, that ought to become Christian, Catholic and Roman, Rome the See and centre of Christ's Unity. To make concessions over, yield, give up the least little bit of our Romanity could never be thought of. »

That Italians could think of it, or rather that Italians *could have this thought of for them,* has seemed so tremendous up there in the land of the Vikings that a certain Swede, author of a well-known « epistle » *To be or not to be* addressed to you, has written a manifesto to the Italians, in Latin, expressing his amazement, together with the Czecho-Slovak Communists, the English and American Protestants and others, and suggesting that, if Latin lands are to give up Latin, it will have to be for the Northern « barbarians » now to make up for it.

Something like this was implied, too, the other day, when the negro President of Senegal, Mr Senghor, on a visit to Rome, delivered his speech on arrival in Latin, at a time when Italy's parliamentarians were busy banishing it from the schools, in sentences of crude, ungrammatical Italian.

The same Swedish writer, from his Northern fastness of ice and snow, has sent us the following tender and mystical definition of Latin: « *Pelicanus est ille myticus, pio fodicat qui pectora rostro datque fervidum sanguinem bibendum et carnem edendam pullis scilicet nobis filiolis atque semper idem et unus manet, non extenuatus, non confectus,* » (*) which amounts to an unconscious and poetic paraphrase of Pius XI, quoted previously: « *...sermonem... universalem, immutabilem, non vulgarem* » — bringing us back to you, your Eminence, and your wringing the Pelican's neck by taking Latin away from the people, smiling, if not laughing, at our « sentimental » standpoint, yet bountifully conceding that what gives you, self-confessed innovator by vocation, annoyance, may all the same be understandably pleasing to others.

Is there not, finally, more said than appears in the short but telling letter sent by the faithful of Norway to their Bishops (letter published in *Musicae sacrae ministerium*, Rome 1967): « Our Bishops having asked us lay people to make our views known on the reforming project of the Church's liturgy, we beg to express the following ideas: —

« We are much troubled by the modifications envisaged in the liturgy of the Mass and particularly the « reform of the language ».

(*) It is the mythical pelican who, wounding her breast, with loving beak gives her young — us children — her own warm flesh and blood to eat and drink, whilst remaining ever one and the same, neither weakened nor spent.

« ... Belonging to Western European culture
and taking account of the Norwegian mentality and
tradition, we are convinced that the use of Latin
in the invariable Mass texts, also apart from the
Canon, remains ever as precious and useful as
formerly.

« For love of the Roman Catholic Mass we
sincerely desire that those who have the weighty
mission of defending such great values give proof
of a real discernment and deep piety. »

FOREIGNERS ALSO IN CHURCH

Quoting us as asking if then Latin, the Church's
language, by which the Catholic Church is felt to
be one throughout the world, is to be abandoned
for the vernacular, your generosity went to the
lengths of assuring us our consternation was appreciated (thank you, your Eminence!). You even
professed a degree of rhetorical indignation yourself at the idea that a whole heritage of Gregorian
chant, classical polyphony and later sacred music
composed to Latin texts and requiring Latin should,
after centuries, be set aside or consigned to arch-
ives. As for sacred architecture, if our churches,
even our great churches, with due deference to Bra-
mante, Michaelangelo, Bernini, Pugin and others,
have not hitherbo been built in the most « functional » manner (implying it was time they
were corrected — but with « greatest prudence »,
naturally — in regard to « community sense », that
is without any offending « diaphragm » of columns,

pillars, naves, etc., etc., getting in the way between the « assembly » and the single central altar, Protestant-wise) you magnanimously concede these churches, nevertheless, also stand for an « artistic heritage » not to be despised. *But* you say — and here comes your *but* in regard to all — « compared with all these things, sound enough in themselves, there is something greater : the communicating to these people of God's Word in a way that they can understand and take in, the bringing of them close to the altar so that they may consciously participate in the assembly of the family of God. »

This word « assembly » — « family » is harmless enough — is objectionable : it makes one think of a club, just what preachers and instructors intent on instilling into Catholics greater awareness and conscientious membership have hitherto stressed the Church is *not*. The words smacks of the co-op. — of popular co-ownership, co-government. But what makes one's blood boil is not necessarily that, but the disregard you here show *for the Church* — from lack of reflection only, let us hope, remembering your above-quoted conference was given during the Carnival, your street games and confetti-throwing may have distracted you. For if logic still avails — if even *that* has not been reformed in your part of the words — the conclusion to be drawn from your words is that, previous to you, the great reforming legislator and de-Latinizer of the liturgy, the Church with all her popes, saints, doctors and liturgists (from Pope St. Damasus to Cardinal Schuster) was wide of the mark, was getting in the way as to the People of God's spiritual development and progress, still further culpable for having fostered and defended Latin when those capable of mastering it were a very few educated persons mostly of the higher classes, whereas now nearly all have some education and a great many are in a position to learn and understand it without undue hardship — *especially the Latin peoples!*... Nor was there in former times available the help of bilingual missals — Latin-Italian, Latin-French, Latin-Spanish, Latin-English, Latin-German — which do not go down well with you at the present time (except possibly the one brought out by Fr Bugnini) since for you they get in the way, like the great Latin « diaphragm », between altar and assembly, between priest-president and assembly of people. These missals are really the exact opposite of a dividing line, enabling Latin, as they do, to be followed to the greatest possible extent by Catholics from South America to New Zealand.

In a seaside town I know in Italy it has always been a wonderfully moving experience at Sunday morning Mass to hear holiday visitors from many lands praying together with us, though in a variety of accents, praying as one, especially at the Crede, the *Et unam, sanctam, catholicam et apostolicam Ecclesiam,* pronounced or sung by them in foreign surroundings with noticeable awareness and feeling. How sad, on the other hand, it has been, these last couple of years, to see the same visitors no longer at home in one and the same Catholic sacred building, forced now to stand aloof — those, that is, who have the courage to enter, many staying outside, missing Mass — eyeing one another and us without being able to understand a word, aware only of being foreigners, and of what has changed. Here is something far more isolating than mere columns and naves in sacred architecture. A British ex-officer and one-time pris-

óner of the Germans, told me he remembered how
neither the barbed-wire, concentration camp walls
nor sentinels could prevent a feeling of freedom
on Sunday morning when, in the midst of all, the
German Catholic chaplain signed himself at the
foot of the altar and he heard the opening words
of the Mass — *Introibo ad altare Dei* — as it might
have been his parish priest in London. Nor can I
forget the tearful face of an old lady, a convert
from Protestantism, above all on account of what
she had seen and realised abroad of the Church's
mark of unity in worship and language — the *Ut
unum sint* which now, in the name of another unity
and universality, you and yours are setting about
destroying, bit by bit.

MARTHA AND MARY

Unity, in fact, has gone. Unity of language vanished, unity of hearts has disappeared too — even
between the people of one and the same parish,
region, religious community, family. Everywhere
unity has given place to discussion, disagreement,
self-opinionatedness and division. Often, where
unity is still apparent, it is only because many are
silent, not daring to speak, or thinking it more
prudent, for the time, not to do so in public.
Outwardly, most of the clergy feel they have no
choice but to conform, out of obedience. But dare
I ask you, your Eminence, if among your own
priests and religious brethren there is really more
love for one another than before? Most certainly
it is not so, as you must be well aware, among the

clergy in general, as also between the new breed priests and nuns, and those that have remained as they were. Your « reform » has, as is well known, even resulted in open rebellion here and there, on the part of people who are not afraid to call a thing by its true name, and rightly call this *a change of religion*. With us in Italy, in the Upper Adige region, and in Istria, for example, the Mass, until recently celebrated in the language of all (because of none in particular) was the only thing that kept all united. Now that has been nationalised, already existing differences, sharpened and soured, are provoking brawls, sometimes in sacred precincts, requiring the presence of armed police : so that your « Go in peace! » in place of the last Gospel amounts in actual practice to the injunction « Off with you and have it out among yourselves outside! »

In Britain, one is informed, the difficulties already existing among non-Catholics of the national observance, for example because of the difference between Welsh spoken in the North, and in the South, have become part of a Catholic « language problem » (it is evidently now the thing for Christ's Church to « have headaches » with everyone else).

In Spain, with the authorisation in 1966 of the Preface of the Mass in Castilian or Catalan (translations in Basque and Galician anticipated) agitation at once began for a « Valencian Mass » (dialect of Catalan), opposed by the local archbishop as « politically motivated » — which, true or not, certainly politicised the dialect in the eyes of others. Notwithstanding, Mr Gerald Bryan, writing in the London *Tablet*, recounted humorously how, on account of the remarkable microphone technique achieved by the officiating priests, he left one church of the Valencian region none the wiser as to whether he had heard Mass in Castilian (Spain's official national vernacular), the Valencian dialect, or Latin!...

Then there were the unruly disputes last year at Louvain university, reported truly enough as no longer being about religion, as in the 16th century, but over a *language*, Catholic Flemish students thinking it an honour to fight side by side with Protestants against the *French-speaking* populace, although in the bilingual city of Ghent the cultural language has been French for centuries. The public flouting of Bishops' authority, the scandalous scenes and sacrileges committed in sacred places during religious ceremonies, were a reminder of religion's having been subordinated, as with Protestantism, to nationalistic and political interests, when not being used to further them.

See how they do not love one another! could today be said of us by modern pagans; and here is but one of the bitterest fruits, among the many delusive ones, of a reform launched in the name of communal worship, community spirit etc., in reality more in the manner and spirit of Communism than Catholic Communion, from which the Communists took the word — reform aiming to abolish « caste » and « dividing lines. »

In France one read of the Bishops of Brittany setting up interdiocesan commissions to fix texts in the « noble and elevated language » of the Breton dioceses, and of their giving guidelines in regard to the use of Breton and French in the Mass, the most suitable solution being « One Sunday in French, the next in Breton »; and for the Sacraments, Baptisms and marriages, « the faithful choosing the language they prefer » (democratically — except, needless to say, Latin, a request for which is regretfully, often bluntly, turned down). It is worth noting, that all the reforms, down to the latest of the Canon being celebrated « in the living language », meet with the benevolent and publicised approval of the noted Protestant community of Taizé

In India, with her still surviving two hundred languages (and calendars) Bishops across whose dioceses run the borderlines of several different language regions have been obliged to readopt the Roman Latin Missal for all and with which all were formerly satisfied, when not inveigled into thinking otherwise, to avoid embarrassment for themselves and their clergy, as well as racial and politically coloured squabbling at the altar-rail.

In another part of the world, South Africa, we find Catholics now hotly arguing in print whether the coloured people prefer Afrikaans in the Mass, or English; and reports come in of scenes of Bedlam, making even hard-boiled vernacularists tear their hair, one half an « assembly » responding in English, the other half simultaneously in Afrikaans — just to show how they *feel*. It is known, besides, that many African dialects do not contain words equivalent to those used in the Roman liturgy at all, so that a whole new set would have to be invented by the local *académie africaine* — with what traditional procedure and dogmatic fidelity to the original true meaning may be left to the imagination.

Una Voce recently published a detailed report from Professor Retamal-Favereau on the situation in South American Chile where, at first by fits and starts, almost imperceptibly, then suddenly with a rush despite feeble and unorganised protestation, the changes have been carried through, mostly by the parish priests and different religious superiors, without coordination, resulting in a chaotic state of affairs: altars turned round or tables substituted, Tabernacles removed, various « Chilean Masses » composed and performed of unutterable mediocrity and devoid of the spirit of religion. Inspite of the contempt of the people themselves, these national Masses have the support of many of the clergy — but not all. In some churches, kneelers have altogether been removed to prevent the people going down on their knees, now held to be a « slavish posture ». Priests have been known to shout at Communicants who kneel to stand up, out of respect for Christ, and continue shouting as they advance with the Host in their hands. Those who oppose the « new way of praying » are harshly rebuked in sermons, and called « modern Pharisees, hypocrites and whited sepulchres, » or (most like the pot calling the kettle black) « neo-Protestants. » Mass is celebrated by extremists round a common table, as though the rite consisted in nothing more than a repetition of the Last Supper, the Crucifix supplanted by a microphone so that the words of the common language, such as for example « the shortened Credo », may not fail to enter every ear. Latin is almost everywhere execrated, and scarcely heard. The Benedictines and Franciscans, amongst others, have made abortive attempts to introduce Gregorian to Spanish words, soon abandoned on discovering the truth that Gregorian can only be sung to Latin. Irreverence, iconoclasm and eccentricities of all kinds are the order of the day, and a spirit of arrogance that brooks no correction. With all this, apart from a general lessening of devotion, church attendance has not increased in numbers; instead, not a few, horrified and disconcerted, have given up their religious practices. Professor Retamal-Favereau's report ends, notwithstanding, on a note of hope, that these things may serve to make apparent the urgent need for a return to the ancient forms and customs which have given proof of their spiritual value and efficacy for so many centuries.

Let us now come to Rome, where, during the Octave of prayer for Christian Unity, an English Catholic who for years had regularly attended the celebrations at the Church of the Gesù, last year entered on the evening dedicated to the return of Anglicans to hear the Mass being sung to a strange, tuneless and amorphous incantation, in Italian. Enquiring of the usher, a young layman eager to hand him the Unity prayer leaflet inside the door, why Mass for the return of Anglicans to the universal Church was being sung in the national language of Italy in the midst of Catholic Rome, the pert, offhand retort came swiftly: « We are all Italians *here!* » Well — the other usher happened to be a negro Atonement Brother; all around were sprinklings from Rome's different national colleges of every hue and dress, American, Irish, Scots, Germanic, and many others; the servers on the altar were all from the English College... and that Unity Mass painfully dragged on, to the tune of Three Blind Mice and variations not-so-various, before hundreds of « dumb spectators » if ever they were so, in *Italian!...* Nor was there any mistaking the changed atmosphere in the church which, from having been formerly always full to overflowing, was now three quarters only. And that evening there was *one* Englishman less...

Even in St. Peter's, where but two Masses may be celebrated in the vernacular on Sundays, at 9 a.m. and noon, it is not uncommon for people quietly and attentively following a low Mass at one or other of the side altars to find the celebrant suddenly break off from Latin into American, or German, often at the *Agnus Dei* and actual moment of

Communion, shattering union and setting up linguistic, nationalistic and jarring disunited thoughts and feelings, the excuse being that « permission » has been granted for a national group, frequently conspicuous for its absence, the « permission », one suspects, as often as not having been got only in theory. At such moments, intending Communicants, inspite of themselves, unable or perhaps unwilling to overcome feelings of indignation, not to say outrage, have been seen to turn away with hurt or angry faces, without receiving.

You and your pragmatic, progressive, anti-Latinizers, your Eminence, deign to offer consolation and reassurance by conceding that Latin is still all right — *useful* — at « international gatherings » — meaning Lourdes, Fatima, international Eucharistic Congress, and conferences. This would imply, granting Latin the right to live on certain occasions, that only here and on these occasions is the Catholic Church now universal and international, that it is ordinarily and in other places and on other occasions national; when the truth as everyone really knows is that the Church is always and in every place and on every occasion not only international but supernational, and never more than in the Mass, central act of worship obliging all the Church's members.

Perhaps — may the prophet pardon the ass this also! — sufficient prayer and meditation have been lacking to most upright intentions in all these things. And might not more meditation and prayer have indeed shown how tragically ridiculous it is (not my words but those of a Bishop correspondent) that an age so out of joint, so off its head and of so little faith as ours, should presume to set itself up as teacher to the nineteen centuries before it, for the most part far more Christian in every way than our own? Well, if prayer and piety are useful to all, here is surely a case of going down on one's knees and staying there until they are sore. « I believe more in prayer than in medicines », said Michaelangelo, who raised St. Peter's dome to the Roman sky, in his humble faith. Bernanos was saying much the same thing, it seems, when he exclaimed, about reforms, « The Church has less need of reformers than of *saints.* » Yes, *the Church needs Mary more than Martha.* This is the exact opposite of what is being taught today, as thought Christ had said: « Mary, Mary, you pray too much! » and had praised the other.

Good Pope John, when they tried to convince him that the increased tempo and exigences of modern life required a certain sacrifice of prayer, for the sake of action, replied by drawing out his Rosary, with the words: « As far as I am concerned, I make a point of saying the fifteen Mysteries every day. » John XXIII evidently saw, in today's scant will to pray, the reason for asking curtailment of the Breviary, something you have granted to a greater extent than was asked, cutting down the Davidic Hours from seven to four, as well as giving up a number of the most beautiful hymns and mutilating the Psalter, no longer said in its entirety — except by some priests (and lay people) who, precisely on account of life's greater intensity and exigency today, have *increased* prayer, still making their preparation before Mass, as well as their thanksgiving after, although no such prayer or instructions are any more to be found in your « reformed » Missals.

« WE ARE NOT CONVERTING, BUT BEING CONVERTED »

Certain it is that when the mission of the twelve Apostles — that of *reforming the world* — grew to proportions they could no longer deal with themselves alone, they did not put aside, or shorten, their « Breviary ». They delegated « social welfare » questions (as we say today) to others, specially appointed deacons: « It is not reason that we should leave the Word of God and serve tables » (says the Acts of the Apostles) « but we will give ourselves continually to prayer and to the ministry of the Word. » As a consequence, « And the Word of the Lord increased; and the number of disciples was multiplied in Jerusalem exceedingly. »

Nothing similar is either seen or promised in the manner or method of your « reform ». The contrary is happening, Catholics ceasing to grow, even beginning to diminish (the Jesuit General not long ago gave figures that should cause alarm). As for the « separated brethren », we have seen how they so far have shown less and less inclination to come towards us since we appear to have lost the courage and the conviction to show them theirs is not the right path, and ours the right one. Every day one hears and reads of the need for reunion on both sides; never once does one hear or read it clearly affirmed « in the one, true Catholic Church of Christ » — although Paul VI has many a time at general audiences and on other occasions spoken against the perils of a « post-conciliar mentality », relativism, irenicism, the watering down of Catholic beliefs and practices in the hope of pleasing and gaining others. Such weakness, human respect, opportunism and half measures neither please, attract nor convince anyone. None are converted. Many, not only among those in search of the truth and certainty, but also among those already having it, are scandalised, repelled and disgusted. One even read in the papers, but could hardly believe it was not a misprint, or erroneous reporting, concerning the « dialogue » undertaken at Strasbourg between the Catholic Church and the Lutheran World Federation, that by « dialogue » « both delegations understand *the common search for truth... pursued on a footing of equality.* » The Catholic Church, *Mater et Magistra,* Mother and Teacher of peoples, searching for truth (which she *is*) and on the same level as those wilfully separated from her, and in error — blind guide of the blind!...

And by the way one notes the words *conversion* and *convert,* lest they offend the ears of any, have by your Eminence, in the name of reform, been struck out from your Missal, and from the solemn ecumenical impetrations of the Friday of the Passion — though you shed crocodile's tears over this, nonetheless: « It is with regret » (Fr Bugnini is speaking) « that we have to lay hands upon certain venerable texts which have for centuries so efficaciously nurtured Christian piety, and which still today have the aura of the heroic ages of the Church's dawn. » And « It is hard, » Fr Bugnini elsewhere has admitted, « to retouch literary works of art of a power and conception that are unsurpassable. » The same delicacy of feeling is shown in regard to atheists. « No battle with atheism! » declares the Secretariate for non-believers. Same deference towards Communism — towards all and sundry. And if these tactics elicit any reaction from them whatever, it is that we Catholics appear to be overdoing it, making an exhibition of ourselves, in these concessions, to the extent of leaving *them* to make the conditions, be the first to fix the price of reunion and reconciliation. « Certain subjects must first be more carefully gone into, » a Communist Congress has concluded. « The confessional schools, divorce, etc... »

To come back to the Protestants: « You mean to meet us, but in this way you nauseate us! » one has heard some of the sects say in Italy. As for the Anglicans, who, since the Archbishop of Canterbury was the first Church leader to propose praying for the successful outcome of the Ecumenical Council, might be considered among the best disposed, if not the nearest, it will be remembered how Dr Ramsey was publicly petitioned, before going to Rome, to *beware of inviting the Pope to London if he had at heart the present atmosphere of charity and tolerance among Christians of different denominations* — that is, the interconfessionalism or pan-Christianity in which the other side considers their ecumenism, and ours, ought to merge (dissolve would be a better word) judging from the published prediction of his Grace in Jerusalem last year to the effect that « there will one day be a Holy Orthodox Catholic Church of which all Christian Churches will be a part, providing for the continued existence of autocephalous Churches. This would be consistent with Christian unity. » Perhaps the International Church of One Religion, whose central multi-million-dollar temple is being built in America, will be a future heretical rival. Referring, anyway, to the postponement of voting on the conciliar decree *De Libertate* at the Council, Canon Bernard Pawley, Canterbury's former Rome representative, quoted with approval a remarkable statement in the Anglican *Church Times* apropos of this: « ...after so many centuries of error in the matter (religious liberty) it does not seem to us to be of great moment if the declaration of the official conversion of the Roman Church is delayed by a few months. » « But of the conversion itself », Canon Pawley himself ended, « there can be no doubt. »

Conversion? « *We are not converting, but being converted* »... opined already one who was then Cardinal Archbishop of Milan. « Instead of affirming our own ideas compared to others, the others' ideas are being accepted. We are not conquering, but surrendering. Old friends who have stayed in the right path are being called reactionaries, and those capable of every weakness and compromise are esteemed true Catholics. » If this is indeed the case, concerning the word « reactionaries », we Catholics holding to the Catholic language know it with particular acuteness; for on that very account we are called reactionaries, and as such deprecated, disliked, fought by your *avant-garde*, your Eminence. And, were this not to our honour, we might almost be envying the atheists, Mahometans, Buddhists, Hebrews, Masons, Marxists, Modernists and heretics of all kinds who are your real brethren, we the half-brothers — we, now, the separated ones. We are now the Church of Silence (without posing as martyrs, but certainly, as I do here, *reacting*), having now no say in any of the so-called Catholic papers, in which the *de Libertate* holds good only for those who conform to your progressive, modernising, de-Latinizing, desacralizing, communizing policies.

The other day, while travelling with a priest friend who wanted to celebrate in Latin (it was a Sunday morning) and applying at a large church of the city where we broke our journey, we were told we could have an altar in the crypt, if we liked, *where nobody would know of it.* There I served the Mass of my friend, reminded forcibly enough of the catacombs, but cheered considerably, as the priest was, by the presence of a number of others who, word having got round that there was « a real Mass » being said underground, had come to take part, with visible relief and satisfaction.

THE FAITH OF THE HUMBLE

Conversions, it was said, no longer take place. Rather is it perversions that are to be seen all around us. So allow me, your Eminence, in this regard to transcribe as though it were my own view another passage of the theologian already quoted previously in regard to the « dialogue » with the reformed Lutherans and their progeny, that holds good also for your Reform: Here is the conclusion he came to after a study of the various attempts made at regaining the « separated » by means of conversations on an equal footing — from the dispute beween John Eck and Andrew Carlostadio of 1519, to the Malines conversations of the first postwar period: « These historical precedents forbid us to give way to rosy views on the subject of the reunion of the churches on the rock set by Christ... To expect the heads of heresies to climb down from the positions that they have maintained for centuries has always seemed to me Utopian. One must be prepared to wait patiently, centuries if necessary, for conversions of the people together, not awaiting these as a result of theological argument, but imploring them with the faith and tears of St. Monica from Him who holds the hearts of men in His hands. »

The faith and tears of the humble — of St.

Monica... which amounts to saying, the *prayer of humility*, fundamentally needed: « *Nisi Dominus*... Unless the Lord build the House, they labour in vain who build it... » And first of all it is necessary that a man labour on his *own* building, at his own conversion, without which it is worse than useless, crass pride, to pretend to work for the conversion of others. But it does not seem to me that on such a foundation of prayer, self-improvement and *humility* rests « the people's spiritual formation » vaunted by your reforming policies. I say the prayer of humility, underlining the qualifying substantive, for it would be effrontery for me to doubt, even with you, the great innovator, that prayer 'were at the base of this « spiritual .formation ». Yet, the word's *never once* having escaped your lips during all your reiterated perorations and inculcations publicising your reform could give one reason to wonder. Also, as your lieutenants are fond of saying, echoing you, doubtless, after March 7th 1965, one no longer goes to church to pray the Mass, one goes « to make a community action », rather as one should visit the local pub. where, besides bread and cheese and beer, light electronic music is not lacking — or perhaps to the parish hall for a « love feast », at which the « liturgy of the word » accompanies food and drink and singsong.

What humbug! For you, the church has become the House of prayer to the exclusion of Latin — but the Mass *is* prayer — the prayer of prayers. The prayer you believe in, though, is not the prayer of the humble, the prayer of St. Monica. It is the kind of prayer that resembles the hideous, bare, cold, collective, mystery-lacking new churches your school of liturgy is erecting — more like assembly rooms, sports stadiums or lecture halls than churches — in which prayer mechanical, regimented, rationalised must be « understood » by everyone, with the help of light and sound apparatus, electronic ambos and cabins cluttering up the sacred precincts and sanctuary, where there is one. Instead of virtue and humility you have set up Reason, intellect: « If I don't understand, I don't pray » you are trying to make people think, and many are now, parrot-like, repeating it. Is this the best way of drawing nearer to Christ, Who said: « I thank Thee, Father, that Thou has hidden these things from the wise, and intellectual, and hast revealed them to little ones »?

It is surely not what the saints have taught us, either, from holy writ or from their own writings and example. « *Quoniam non cognovi litteraturam introibo in potentias Domini* », the psalmist says again, and he knew something of literature, as did the great St. Teresa of Avila, mystic and poetess, who chose for her spiritual advantage and devotion to remain in ignorance on certain matters. The reformer of Carmel, she has left it on record that the more some things remained obscure to her, the more she believed them and felt an increase of devotion... « *màs firme la tenìa, y me dava devociòn grande...* » continung: « I did not even wish to understand them ...the more difficult things are to the intelligence, the more they inspire me with devotion. » (*)

God resists the proud, and gives His grace to the humble. And it has always been the humble who have served God in accomplishing His great things, beginning with the humble handmaid, His Mother, and His carpenter foster-father, neither of whom understood the things He told them — *non intellexerunt* — in the Temple! So much for under-

---

(*) *Life of St. Teresa.*

standing everything. Bernadette Soubirous was not, we know, the brightest girl in the parish, or in cate-chism class; yet Our Lady appeared to her, and not to the nuns who taught her and treated her as a dunce. Quite a number of people were brought back to God — special trains had in the end to be scheduled for pilgrims to Ars and its Curé — by one since made the model saint and patron of parish priests who would hardly have thought of himself as an intellectual, and who in fact for lack of « intellect » was only just passed by his superiors for the priesthood. And we find the word « blockhead » used in a letter from the Rector of St. Gregory's, in the Venetian region, to the parish priest about a certain young seminarian whom he should on that account dissuade from returning to the seminary after the holidays. But the block-head went back nonetheless, and became in time Fr Angelo Roncalli... and with still more time, at 78, Pope John XXIII, who once recalled, in a con-versation with the Jesuit General, a humble lay brother of the Order, a doorkeeper, whose only book was his Rosary. So much for intellect. Times have changed; but human hearts have not, nor have men's minds, as to all that is needful to them *for the one thing necessary*: their eternal salvation. Which reminds me of a « Mass » I had the misfortune to be present at some while ago, during which, in the midst of the commands pe-remptorily bellowed at the congregation — sorry, assembly — by the curate like any sergeant-major to the company on parade — Sit!... Stand!... Kneel!... Sing! *All together!*... the rite was solemnly interrupt-ed to order an old lady to « put that thing away » — *that thing* being her Rosary, which, scarcely able to bear the new way of praying any more, she had taken out of her bag and clasped in her hands, to give her courage — in the eyes of the new-breed curate a more heinous act than producing lipstick and powder in church, and applying it.

« If I don't understand, I don't pray. » Somewhat the equivalent of St. Thomas's « Unless I see.. » — though he was unbelieving more from excess of love than anything. And an equivalent reply to that of Our Lord could be: « Blessed are they that have not understood, and do not understand, but who have prayed, and continue to pray! »

How many millions and millions down the ages have been buried in our Catholic churchyards with the Rosary, in life their only book, entwined round their joined fingers! — those Rosary beads shown in Michaelangelo's Last Judgement in the Sistine Chapel as little chains clung to by risen beings who are thereby drawn up to Heaven. God grant — if our view is only one of lamentably outmoded sentiment — that a still greater number may be drawn up by those popular Mass leaflets of yours, that greater glory may be given to God by these « new Christians » of yours, who come without *that thing* into your « new functional churches », complete with neon signs and electronic aids, deprived of the Latin « diaphragm », and even of sacred images and statues... But, in the meantime, we do not intend putting *that thing* away. We rejoice, and are even grateful in our ignorance, faithfully following in all things what the Angelic Doctor, St. Thomas Aquinas, wrote in this regard about sacred chant in Latin: « *...etsi aliquando non intelligant quae cantantur, intelligunt tamen propter quid cantentur, scilicet ad laudem Dei; et hoc sufficit ad devotionem excitandam*: even if they do not understand what is sung, they understand why it is sung, that is, in God's praise; and that suffices for arousing devotion. »

THE TORN TUNIC

To be sure you have not spared yourself, your Eminence, in planning to arouse devotion according to these new ways of yours — as you would have it, more beneficial. Proof of this we have, it seems, in your cooperating (gratis, naturally, for who is not aware of your disinterest and magnanimity?) in the sale of a potent « electronic ambo » (patented) manufactured and launched by a big business firm in praise of God at the price of lire 168,000. None familiar with your vocabulary and style could doubt the authorship of the publicity propaganda for this contraption, beside a specimen of which you took care to be photographed before discoursing on its « functional effectiveness. » *Makes possible direct and immediate contact between celebrant, reader or commentator and assembly of the faithful,* so runs the blurb. *Gives due evidence in the liturgy of the word to the reader or commentator in respect to other officiators, even if the latter have mains amplification. Entirely solves amplification problems in small and medium-sized churches, it being possible to connect a second pair of microphones with independent tone and volume control for the celebrant. The electronic ambo is adaptable to any kind of mains amplification and can be suitably operated at will to preserve the particular enhancing qualities of the effective vocal presence of the reader, commentator or celebrant,* so ends this highly lucid legend, with a peculiar flourish, in witness of the fact that, humanly and electronically speaking, you have indeed left nothing undone in your strenuous endeavours to galvanize the populace, and communicate God's Word to them « in such a way that they will understand and be able to absorb it, drawing them near to the altar so that they may be enabled to take *conscious* part in the assembly », and so forth, and so on — a more conscious part than formerly, your Eminence, by means of the « *particular enhancing qualities of the effective vocal presence* » — nearer to the altar and more consciously « participating » than during all the past centuries of humble piety and adoration of the Mystery, veiled by Latin (*vere Tu es Deus absconditus*) and venerable for that very reason — just as the Sacred Species both presént and veil the Sacrament of the Eucharist for us, or as the Holy Rosary and the meditation of its Mysteries tell us all that the altar reminds us of, renews and perpetuates...

May God indeed will things as *you* would have them, if that were more beneficial, and to His greater glory, no matter if it humiliated us Latin-lovers, sentimentalists, traditionalists, esthetes and advocates of beauty. No doubt « a soul is worth more than all Latin put together », as a colleague of yours proclaimed when your March 7th was approaching, although letting us know he did not deceive himself that it would be enough to replace Latin with the everyday language and turn the altar round for the people to come running *en masse* and be converted. But your colleague's first proposition can also be turned the other way round, by stating: « One soul is of more value than all the vernacular... » And over two years' experience of the latter should go to show whether the exchange has been worth it.

Has it?

Well, a reckoning has been called for by several, even among those that are not necessarily of our persuasion religiously but who nevertheless join us in battle from nothing more than a sense of beauty — and beauty and truth can be synonymous, — according to a young poet who died in Rome, neither a Roman nor a Christian, explicitly — that sense of beauty and fittingness which made thousands all over the world, by no means art connoisseurs or even art-lovers, to some extent share in the general trepidation for the safety of Michaelangelo's *Pietà* on its ocean voyage to America, and in the public indignation over the ruffianly scratching not long ago of some of the masterpieces in Florence's Uffizi Galleries. To quote a writer in one of the well-known reviews of Italy: « Since the *pastoral* reasons for the present subversion have been so much boasted it will be only fair and lawful to demand an account of the harvest of conversions reaped by the new liturgy in the vernacular, » the writer adding sceptically, without waiting for an answer: « But who in the world would ever be converted merely because the Authorities have seen fit to bring the Church into line with the Protestant 16th century, after waking up to the fact of Italian having been spoken in Italy for a good thousand years? » Underlining how delicately prayer should be dealt with, its ordinarily *non-discursive, non-rational* character, the fact that prayer rises above and lifts one out of mundane, daily surroundings, needing therefore on many occasions *different-from-every-day expression* (even the early Christians in their major rites *did not use the current vernacular*) the writer returns to the point in question, asking: « What nett result has the Reform in the vernacular so far produced? Has there begun to arise such a host of saints, has such a bevy of miracles been witnessed, as to put to shame those remaining faithful to the Church's Latin tradition?... What have been the first fruits of this liturgical devastation? The faithful ignorant of Latin are to be brought nearer to the Gospel... But have the marring and mutilating of rites and books obtained what bilingual missals, catechism and sermons evidently did not? »

The answer here read between the lines is in the plain fact to hand: *the balance of the last two years gives a clear negative.* Centuries of Latin have not, that anybody knows, alienated a single soul or made charity grow cold in any. But the short period of the vernacular, national and rational liturgy has given rise to the police having to be called to stop brawling in church. It has resulted in Holy Communions being in some places halved, and in many others diminished, whether prospective Communicants have been drilled and dragooned or no. It has made some reduce, others give up, their religious practices. And balance is not a bad word concerning a bartering such as this, which has meant a very good thing financially for some. The plea that the Latin Mass was not understood by the unlettered was also found very convenient, an English priest wrote recently, for the sacrilegious robbers who did well out of the reforming business in the 16th century. As for the doctrinal side, a friend of mine, a man of little faith, admitted he had come near to losing it altogether overhearing the following dialogue between a Catholic priest of ours and a Protestant: Priest: « Each nation now has the liturgy in its own language. » Protestant: « Then you Roman Catholics acknowledge that up to now you have been wrong? » Priest: « Yes. We acknowledge that, up to now, we have been wrong. »

I conclude with the remarks of an American pastor published this year in a U.S. traditional Catholic newspaper: « We were given to understand that the people wanted the new Mass facing the people, but I am convinced now it was the priests who wanted it, not the people... the change has definitely not increased attendance at daily Mass. »

And of another priest, writing in the same paper: « There is one very important thing that the present-day reformers seem to have overlooked: some ninety per cent of the (old Catholic) hymns were designed to inculcate a deep personal love for Christ and His Blessed Mother. That is one of our greatest losses today, and our children are suffering on account of that loss. Another great loss is the lack of reverence; and the « folk Mass » is doing nothing to correct it. *There is no doubt but that the Church today has been infiltrated and the enemy is operating within our ranks.* »

LATIN LANGUAGE OF YOUTH

Is it any wonder that, as the clergy can confirm, Mass attendance and Communions and visits to the Blessed Sacrament have diminished? Since when have grapes been gathered of thorns, or figs of brambles? The wonder would be were there seen the contrary, if this *volte-face*, of language and altar, with the aid of the electronic ambo, had borne the desired spiritual fruits. The wonder would be if this intellectualized, rationalized prayer conditioned to the understanding had proved more acceptable and more greatly answered than the humble prayer of the publican, who would do no more than strike his breast and implore God's mercy. It is indeed immediately after recounting this parable that the Gospel recounts Christ's saying: « Whoever shall not receive the Kingdom of God as a child shall not enter it. »

A child does not have to understand to believe, still less to pray. Understand in order to believe! —

the inverse of St. Augustine's « *Crede ut intelligas!* » — *believe in order to understand!* — principle underlying Augustinian philosophy, so needed in our own day. For only through submitting our intellect to God can we start to understand the mysteries and meaning of existence.

Once again, when the disciples asked Christ direct why He so often spoke in parables, the Master replied: « Because it is given to you to know the mysteries of the Kingdom of Heaven; but it is not given to them. » Let the people — your « true and authentic people » — *understand* what they can — in parables, in Latin, in their own language! But the essential thing is not that they understand, but that they *believe*. Our Lord did not praise any for having understood, but for having believed.

To return to a little matter of *age*, the difficulty « even among the clergy (as you stated) *especially of advanced years* in easily welcoming this reform... » Though age is undeniably and inevitably a contributing factor with those who do not like the new liturgy it is far from being the whole explanation, as you hint. Of course, once you begin to train those of a new generation in the new ideas, they will begin to grow up, for the most part, thinking they are better (until that other school, experience, begins to speak); and it is well known what is freely being taught, from birth-control and Freudian psychology, to pacifism and Marxist philosophy, by anti-Roman, anti-Latin, anti-authoritarian liberal-progressive teachers in some former strongholds of Catholic universities and seminaries. In many, a couple of years ago, the new liturgical ideas, teaching and discipline (or indiscipline) were at first received with protest and dislike; but before long, partly on account of the wish not to go against superiors, the students became resigned. But not all. There are still young seminarians and young members of the clergy who, resisting pseudo-reform and Modernism, are making a true endeavour to renew themselves, and helping others to the same, meeting the needs of the society of their time in accordance with the guidelines of the II Vatican Council. And so also are there many young people, sons and daughters of good, devout, traditional Catholic families who love the Latin Mass and Roman liturgy, the Rosary and true devotions unchangingly, and understand their meaning — unlike the chattering groups, seduced by novelty, seen congregating in church porches on the first Sundays of your « reform », long-haired youths and trousered girls in grotesque get-up, for whom the Mass means no more than a date, assuring themselves and others, to the sound of pocket radio transistors tuned in to beat music, that now for the first time they understood what it was all about.

A Roman school-teacher, determined to see what his own pupils really thought, surprised them one day by asking them direct (without having let them know his own views) which they preferred, the Latin Mass as they had known it, or the new rite. Not only did they spontaneously express a preference for Latin, they also, without being asked, volunteered to say why. And these were some of the reasons quietly and candidly offered for disagreeing with what some of their priests had told them, and even a visiting Bishop: Latin is more mysterious — there is something cold and missing, now — also there is so much noise and confusion it is hard to follow with attention and devotion, and difficult to pray. It's easy for some now to sit on the back benches listening to radio transistors without being noticed. Latin doesn't change, as ordinary language does, in modern times so quickly. Italian is not universal, Latin is... » This gave the teacher the opportunity, at the next English lesson, to tell his pupils of the classical example of total vocabulary-shift in English, King James II's observation on Sir Christopher Wren's new St. Paul's Cathedral: « It is at the same time amusing, awful and artificial » — in present-day parlance pleasing, venerable and done with art. If this is what can happen to the English language, now the most widely used of any, in less than three comparatively slow-moving centuries, what may not occur in two or three modern, fast-moving decades in today's increasingly technical and one world? One's mind goes to a certain cathedral in the Northern hemisphere, recently inaugurated with choreographed Mass ballet-danced round the central altar, the pictures of which resembled a neo-pagan circus-ring in cement, or a multi-gangwayed sports stadium, set for an act of human sacrifice, beneath a sort of inverted spider's webb, with a light-house gone wrong on top: architectural object worthy of King James's words, not in their obsolete but modern sense.

But to come back to young people — when a certain priest of North Italy, claiming to speak for the whole Church, and also a Benedictine liturgical expert and authority in Rome, early this year tried to organise a youth campaign in favour of the vernacular, maintaining all young people are against Latin, 14,000 signatures of young and old were at once collected pro-Latin, as a counter-move and demonstration, in twenty-four hours and only in the Rome diocese.

Is it any wonder then that Latin, *sempervirens*, the language that never grows old, is the ever-young language of the young? *Iuventus, Fides, Robur, Ignis, Albor, Rari nantes, Excelsior, Pro Patria, Virtus, Libertas* are among the names which young people's natural sense of the beautiful and

71

fitting has made them give today, in every country of the world, instead of the corresponding vernacular, to their footbtall teams, racing, swimming, climbing and sporting clubs of all kinds, and which one hears lustily shouted in the world's stadiums.

The latest make of car turned out in America has been christened Secura. Space-flight rivalry has extended the kingdom of the Catholic tongue well beyond *Garamantes et Indos* (Virgil) and *quodcumque terrarum iacet* (Prudentius) launching it beyond the earth into the remotest region yet arrived at by the work of man. And Soviet Russia, with a three-and-a-half-months' course, reached Venus, the bright morning star, one hundred and eight million kilometres distant from our planet, with a missile named *Venus*, though the Russians have a word they could have used, similar enough, *Veniera* — less beautiful and apt than the Latin, « admirable bond of unity » (indeed one would say with Pius XI) in this case *interastral* — some « *diaphragm!* »...

Language of the past as of the present and future, of sport as of dogma, of science and politics (the international doctors' congress held in Prague last year drew up its programme in Latin and UNO has proposed issuing reports in Latin), it is blindness not see in this thoroughly universal language of Rome the universal Church's predestined language. It is — (we dare not use the word) to wish to replace it with the world's language, the Babel of tongues that divide and oppose, and to wish this *today*, just at a moment when the nations, the European ones in particular, are aspiring and working to form a whole, to re-knit together the tunic of their ancient unity, with the favour and blessing of the Church. In the words of Paul VI not long since to the promoters of the European movement: « You know how the Church views with particular sympathy this noble endeavour towards fusion... Spontaneous evolution of life makes of this continent one community... which asks nothing better than to be enlivened by one and the same spirit... » words ill according with those of that conference of yours: « As for the use of the national language we have granted (for Italy) four: French, for the Val d'Aosta; German, for the Upper Adige; Slavonic, for the Julia Venetian region; and Italian for the rest of the country » — at which it was logically asked, then why not Sardinian, Sicilian and the regional languages and dialects of the peninsula, including Neapolitan?

True indeed you do not altogether exclude the logic, and the advantage, of the children of the same Mother praying in one voice to the same heavenly Mother, according to what we read a little time ago in a well-known Catholic newspaper: « United in a common language, all participants from various nations were able to pray together... The moving record of that union of such a number of persons no more divided by the barrier of language but recognising themselves brothers of one and the same family will remain for some time to come indelibly impressed upon the hearts of all... » Indeed!... Only — that « common language », admitted by you with all honours in church, was not Latin, nor even a natural language, but a counterfeit, a robot-tongue — *esperanto* — which out of church, and in other fields, may have its place and be of some service — but there, *in the Mass*, substituting the Church's own, time-honoured, providential and universal language.. that surely suggests the ape of God, Lucifer, the father of lies.

As with esperanto, you have further opened the church doors to jazz, the twist, the tom-tom — *anything but Latin*. Regarding Latin, your rulings are as rigorous as can be: *away with it! — out of church! — out of the Mass! — unless the church be empty and no one sees and hears* — that is (your instructions) « *when the priest says Mass without the presence of the people* », or « *for such Masses as none of the faithful are present at* » — exception made in respect to something slightly scandalous! We personally requested, in the name of that « democracy » and « liberty » you have filled our heads with, that the new vernacular rite be facultative. You flatly denied us. We then asked that on Sunday in churches where several Masses are celebrated (some in Florence have six or seven with international visitors attending) there should be *at least one,* at an advertised hour, in Latin. Even that you refused.

But you are not illogical in this regard. You feared — as we indeed hoped — in granting this, the consequences: a comparison — between what Catholics everywhere have lately loved without question, but which now, having been told they no longer must, they have begun to question. You feared that, seeing and recognising again, and having access to, their beautiful and true Mother, they might think less of and perhaps desert their plain stepmother. It is human enough, your Eminence, that you should think this rite of yours, of your inventing, the more beautiful — even though everyone else, including those (your own friends) that find it « good », unanimously — *una voce* — with us find it hideous. Anyway, with you and your Philistines beauty does not count, or counts so little that we for whom it very greatly counts are slightingly dubbed esthetes, guilty of estheticism.

ESTHETICISM?

To be classed as esthetes in regard to divine worship might be a just reproach if, for love of the outward thing, we were to pay no heed to the inward — were it merely a beautiful façade alluring us without inducing us to go inside — if beauty were not, humanly and spiritually, an incentive to adoration. Have we not seen how the Church's loveliness has attracted, and given her, numberless children?

« *To pray in beauty* », was a motto of Pope Pius X, and he was not an esthete, but a saint. And let us not forget the words of Paul VI to the artists, words voicing the attitude of the Council: « With you, who are in love with beauty, and work for her... the Church has long since made an alliance. You have built and decorated her-temples, celebrated her dogmas, enriched her liturgy... Today, as yesterday, the Church has need of you and turns to you... This world in which we live has need of beauty so as not to suffer shipwreck, in desperation. Beauty, as truth, is what puts joy into men's hearts: it is the precious fruit that resists time's usury, that associates and unites succeeding generations... »

And arrived at this point, that is to say at the Second Vatican Council, let me pause for a further two brief chapters to recall the thought on these matters of two great popes, Pius XII, and John XXIII, who convoked the Council — both pontiffs accorded by the Council the very special honour of their beatification causes being introduced, to the satisfaction of the Catholic world and beyond.

Is it permitted to us, your Eminence, to be of one mind with these Servants of God and Vicars of Christ, whom the Catholic Church hopes to see proclaimed saints?

THE SERVANT OF GOD PIUS XII

Let us, then, ask the Servant of God, Pius XII (whom his successor venerated, hoping for him one day to be proclaimed a Doctor of the Church) what his thought was, and what his will, on the Mass in the vernacular, which in his time the innovators were already making strenuous efforts to use themselves, and have introduced into the Church.

« The rash audacity of those that are deliberately introducing new liturgical usages, or reviving rites already fallen into disuse and not conforming to the laws and rubrics in force, is severely to be reprimanded. Thus, not without great pain, We know that this is taking place not only in minor matters but also in those of very grave importance: there are not lacking, indeed, those that are using the vernacular language in the celebration of the Eucharistic Sacrifice... The use of the Latin language... is a clear and noble mark of unity and an efficacious antidote to all corrupting influences on pure doctrine... » (*Mediator Dei*,

1947) And (in Pope Pius's allocution to the Liturgical Congress of 1956): « It would be superfluous to recall once again that the Church has grave reasons for firmly keeping, in the Latin rite, the unconditional obligation for the celebrating priest to use the Latin language... » Pius XII, speaking of this « obligation », an « *unconditional* » one, says « the Church » requires it, not himself, or the popes; and the first of the many grave reasons for this is implicit in the words with which Pope Pius concluded his severe reminder ordering that what is done in choir « when Gregorian chant accompany the Holy Sacrifice... be done in the Church's language. »

And now let us ask Pius XII — as the Catholic Church is intent on the work of renewal and greater sanctification — regarding his mind on community prayer and personal prayer, expressly concerning « that thing » taken out and used during the Holy Sacrifice. Again from *Mediator Dei*: « The genius, character and inward nature of people are so various and dissimilar as to make it impossible for all to be affected or guided by prayers, singing and sacred actions carried out in common. Furthermore, the needs and dispositions of souls are not alike in all, nor do they remain always the same with individuals. Who, then, is able to say, from such a preconception, that very many Christians are unable to take part in the Eucharistic Sacrifice and reap the benefits? For they can certainly do so in many other ways... as, for example, either by performing acts of piety or offering prayers which, though different in form from the sacred rite, are in conformity with it nevertheless by their very nature... »

We come now to the altar, to the new idea of it — I mean, the altar's function. By altar is not understood, of course, the assortment of substitutes and offensive counterfeits, plywood tables, barrows, counters, soap-boxes and tea-chests tolerated in churches, obstructing and cluttering up the sanctuary, often with centuries-old art-works created and consecrated for worship scrapped, resulting here and there in appeals to the *State*, in the name of art, for the defence of Church worship and decorum. Well, here is what Pope Pius said, listing the deviations championed and attempted by the innovators of the time — re-attempted, rather, for the same old things have been tried, failed and sooner or later been condemned (whether it was 16th century German and English Protestantism, or 17th century Gallicism — Regalism, Rationalism, Jansenism — in France, German Josephism or Italian Leopoldism, all more or less were attempts on the part of princes and temporal powers to gain control over the Church within their kingdoms and regions, and fetter her): « They are not within bounds who would restore the ancient form of table to the altar » (*Mediator Dei*); and to the 1956 Liturgical Congress: « The Council of Trent has declared what disposition of soul it is needful to harbour when in the Presence of the Blessed Sacrament... They who adhere in heart to this teaching do not think of putting forward objections against the Presence of the Tabernacle on the altar... The Person of the Lord must have the central place in divine worship, because it is what unifies the relation between Altar and Tabernacle, conferring upon them their proper meaning... To separate the Tabernacle from the Altar is equivalent to separating two things that, by virtue of their origin and character, must remain united. »

Going on to make explicit reference, in *Mediator Dei*, to the « unlawful Council of Pistoia » (under Leopold of Tuscany) which endeavoured to revive, according to the innovators' methods, « excessive and unsound archaeologism », as well as « efforts to reintroduce the manifold errors that the above Council proposed resulting in great harm to souls and which *the Church* (says Pius XII once more, not the Pope) ever watchful guardian of the deposit of the faith entrusted to her by her divine Founder with good reason condemned », Pius XII concludes: « In fact, such deplorable propositions and initiatives tend to paralyse the sanctifying action by which the sacred Liturgy elevates God's sons by adoption to the Almighty Father, for their salvation... »

Well, your Eminence? What are we to think? Is it conceivable that the II Vatican Council intended to rehabilitate Protestantism, Gallicism, Josephism and the Synod of Leopold? Will you perhaps be petitioning His Holiness Paul VI not to beatify Pius XII, but rather to contradict and condemn him insofar as he was the defender of the abhorred Latin « diaphragm », the upholder of « caste » in church?

THE SERVANT OF GOD JOHN XXIII

Poor, good, saintly Pope John! How hypocritically, perfidiously the Church's enemies held you up as upholding their aims, for the taking in of the ingenuous, and fools! — you who from the outset of your reign clearly condemned « those already condemned by Our Predecessors, in particular Pius XI and Pius XII » (*Ad Petri cathedram*) and their « persecution which for several decades has been pitilessly enforced in many lands, even those of ancient civilisation ». (*Mater et Magistra*). But I do not speak only of these, the Church's openly avowed enemies, whose diabolical duplicity well knew how to take advantage of your goodness and charity — goodness and charity of a saintly man towards the erring, making it out to be acquiescence in error; I speak also of others, your Catholic « friends », whose words and actions concur not with the magisterium of the Church, their Mother and Teacher, of which you were the visible Head, but with her calumniators and persecutors... However, without digressing further, let me return to my main purpose, that of asking John XXIII what was asked of his predecessors, in particular Pius XII — and asking here means also *reminding*, since the relative document, though so recent and of such weight, has been if not deliberately ignored then by very many entirely forgotten.

The Apostolic Constitution *Veterum Sapientia*, on *Latin, Language of the Church*, concerning the promotion and study of Latin, was one of such importance for its Author, that, for the signing and promulgating of it, he chose St. Peter's Basilica and the Feast Day of St. Peter's Chair, February 22nd 1962 — a few months before the opening of the Council convoked « *ad Christiani populi unitatem assequendam confirmandamque.* »

This speaks for the Pope's love towards the object of this document, which consists of nothing other than the most devoted and ardent defence and presentation of Latin, « the Church's own tongue perpetually united to the Church. »

Summing up and making his all that had been said in praise of Latin in bygone centuries by his predecessors, *the last two, Pius XI and Pius XII*, in particular, Pope John sees this tongue as « *loquendi genus pressum, locuples, numerosum, maiestatis plenum et dignitatis* », in its splendour « *quasi quaedam praenuntia aurora Evangelicae Veritatis* », not without the will of God « *non sine di-*

vino consilio », which the Church made hers « *ut quae et nationes omnes complexu suo contineat, et usque ad consummationem saeculorum sit permansura, sermonem sua natura requirit universalem, immutabilem, non vulgarem* »: a language, therefore, « *quam dicere catholicam vere possumus* », « *perpetuo usu consecrata* », « *thesaurus incomparandae praestantiae* », « *vinculum denique peridoneum, quo praesens Ecclesiae aetas cum superioribus cumque futuris mirifice continetur,* » impartial language consolidating different parts, « *cum invidiam non commoveat, singulis gentibus se aequalem praestet; nullius partibus foveat, omnibus postremo sit grata et amica...* » Not being able to transcribe the whole document, described by *Monitor Ecclesiasticus* as « *praeclarissimo documento* » and « cornerstone of the Church's teaching concerning Latin », we pass on to the conclusion, in practice, which is no less clear and definite:

« *Quibus perspectis atque cogitate perpensis rebus...* these things maturely considered and weighed, in the full awareness of Our office and of Our authority, *certa Nostri muneris conscientia et auctoritate*, We decree and order, *statuimus atque praecipimus*:

1. Bishops and Superiors-General of religious Orders shall be at pains to ensure that in their seminaries... where adolescents are trained for the priesthood, all shall studiously observe the Apostolic See's decision in this matter and obey these Our prescriptions most carefully.

2. In the exercise of their paternal care they shall be on their guard — *paterna sollicitudine caveant* — lest anyone under their jurisdiction, being eager for innovation — *novarum rerum studiosi* — write against the use of Latin whether in the teaching of the higher sacred studies or in

sacred rites — *contra linguam Latinam sive in altioribus sacris disciplinis tradendis sive in sacris habendis ritibus usurpandam scribant* — or through prejudice attempt to belittle the Holy See's will or interpret it in their own way. »

Well, what must we make of it, your Eminence? By your own admission, and even boast, you are, *in hac re*, an « innovator » — and what and innovator! — against Latin (which it was incumbent on you to defend) impugning it not with your pen only, but with a truncheon, chasing it out of church. What are we to make of it, your Eminence? For either the Pope (Pope John) was mistaken, with Pius XII, and Pius XI, and all their predecessors (and one recalls how Pope John was adamant in telling certain religious Superiors *to turn out of their monasteries and convents any who had a bee in their bonnet about Latin*), or it is you that are mistaken.

Please do not make answer with some relativism, such as that a pontifical act, or act of a particular pontiff, as deliberated and weighty as *Veterum Sapientia*, may be of less value and power than a popular song — or that the Council Fathers, after burying, with tears, the Pope who convoked the Council, immediately proceeded, dry-eyed, to go back upon the document whose ink had scarcely been blotted and which he had left to the Church « *ad perpetuam rei memoriam* » with this final intimation: « ...and in virtue of Our Apostolic Authority, We will and command that all the decisions, decrees, proclamations and recommendations of this Our Constitution remain firmly established and ratified, notwithstanding anything to the contrary however worthy of special notice... *contrariis quibuslibet non obstantibus, etiam peculiari mentione dignis.* »

THE COUNCIL

The Council, despite the Devil's crafty attempts to intrude horns and tail, was faithful to Pope John, as Pope John to all his predecessors. It is not the fault of the Council if the liturgical legislation emanating from it has resulted in a perverted application, detested alike by Catholics and non-Catholics, believers and unbelievers, in the name of piety, unity, concord, art, poetry, and beauty.

Far from having banished Latin — as is widely believed and repeated by priests and laity who keep on speaking of reform but without any reference to the Constitution on the Liturgy, and often without ever having read it — the Council reconfirmed Latin as the language of the Church's divine worship in clear and lapidary terms, as: Article 36. *Linguae latinae usus in ritibus latinis servetur* — the use of the Latin language, in Latin rites, is to be maintained. This is therefore the *rule*, as is logically confirmed in the next paragraph beginning, *Cum tamen*, admitting the possibility of limited exceptions: « Supposing, however, that... not infrequently, *haud raro*, the use of the vernacular language may be found very useful for the people, its introduction is granted in part, especially in readings and admonitions, and in certain prayers and singing, *in lectionibus et admonitionibus, in nonnullis orationibus et cantibus...* There is the same *faculty* (not obligation or even recommendation, but rather the repetition of a limitation) in article 63: « In the administration of the Sacraments it is lawful to use, *adhiberi potest*, the vernacular language. » The expressions « Supposing that... », « it is granted that... », « in certain prayers... », « it is lawful... », all go to show *limited* *exceptions* of what has been laid down as the sovereign and general rule. And I ask, we Catholics ask who are still Roman, and not Felsinan (*) how it has been possible so largely to abuse so little power, to the extent in actual fact of turning the Constitution the other way round, making the rule the exception and the exception the rule, and not only the rule but the prohibition of what has been expressly ordered by your obligatory exclusion of Latin for all, except to tolerate it in a Mass « said without the presence of the people », when, that is, no faithful are present, but only the pews.

It is true there *was* a certain *Instructio ad exsecutionem Constitutionis de Sacra Liturgia recte ordinandam »* (of *your* confection, not the Council's, in which the *recte* was understood in an exactly opposite sense, making the Instruction a *de*struction); and this gave you the means for side-stepping the rule and still more reducing Latin by extending the lawfulness of the vernacular throughout the Mass, almost. But also here you yourself made a condition, that places should be taken into account. I am sure I do not know whom you had in mind — Hottentots, Zulus, the Mau-Mau, Red Indians? — any but the inhabitants of the land of Cicero and Virgil, where *to speak Latin* still means, in popular parlance, *to speak plainly*. And yet, on the contrary, because of the number of dialects and the impossibility of expressing certain concepts in them at all, the missionaries in many regions have had no choice but to keep up the Latin liturgy. (As for the brazen assertion, flaunted by a certain liturgical « expert » at a Council press conference, and published in the world Catholic press, that the immutability of Latin is a myth, as « al-

---

(*) Felsina = Bologna (Etruscan name).

though Latin does not change, the meaning of certain words changes... » this is a flagrant contradiction of the words of the Pope, in *Veterum Sapientia* (at the time already published): « Certain Latin words », wrote Pope John, « it is true, acquired new meanings as Christian teaching developed and needed to be explained and defended, but these new meanings have long since become accepted and firmly established. »

I tell you, your Eminence — and I know what I am saying — that not for long will you be able to count upon the kind of obedience professed by the farm labourer who gravely declared to me, after March 7th 1965: « To be sure the Mass suited me better as it was before. But what priest says goes for me and I does as I am told. If priest says I must dance, then dance I will. If priest says I must whistle, then I'll whistle. And if priest says I must croon, then that is what I'll do. »

I saw this good man again not long ago, some time after the disbanding of our parish choir in which we both at one time sang. He had rather changed his tune. « Well, » he said to me, « to be sure, if *this* is what priest wants now, I must say — I don't know... »

"IN GRATIA CANTANTES DEO"

How grand they were indeed, those sung Masses! And the thought of the loss of them is so mournful a thing as to remind one of Babylon... *By the waters of Babylon we sat down and wept...* the only difference being that these « Babylonians » are not requiring but forbidding us to sing *our* Songs of Zion, making us sing theirs, or be silent. For Babylon now is Bologna — liturgical Bologna in the person of your Eminence — which, alas, as pilot-diocese (*Bononia locuta est*) *docet* — *fait école* for all the others, which meekly and mutely follow like Dante's sheep, doing whatever is done or shall be done there, never asking why or wherefore, or if what is being done should be, yet vaguely recollecting some Constitution or other on the Liturgy of the Bishops in Council — of which there is a chapter VI, concerning music in church, entitled *De Musica Sacra*.

A matter of ten articles by reason of which, really, it must be acknowledged that the Dove was indeed fluttering about St. Peter's during the sacred sessions, keeping at bay the Intruder intent on the ruin of souls; for without doubt through the Council the innovators hoped sacred music would suffer the same fate as they wished for Latin. The proof of this would seem to be from the fact *of not a single musician's having been called to take part in the preparatory Commission,* either for personal reputation or high office held in the field of sacred music — as though it were deemed superfluous to invite doctors to a public health conference even though a number of high repute were at hand. And upon a certain person's thinking this absurd, and demanding the reason, the reply forthcame from the innovators, artlessly enough, *because the ideas of sacred musicians were not theirs.* As cannot be denied.

But notwithstanding these bad beginnings, and the ostracizing of competence and talent, the intention and the effort to make Gregorian chant and polyphony things of the past did not prevail: as for Latin, so for sacred music, the Council declared: *Servetur* — it must stay. Moreover, the first of the ten articles extols it, welcomes it, from the past, for the present, as for the future, calling it *a treasure of priceless worth,* never to be gainsaid or given up by the Church: « *Musica traditio Ecclesiae universae thesaurum constituit pretii inaestimabilis...* » — the musical tradition of the Church is a heritage of inestimable value, excelling amid the other forms of art... » This praise is taken up again in the decreeing paragraph: « *Thesaurus Musicae sacrae summa cura servetur et foveatur...* » — the treasure of sacred music is to be kept and cherished with the utmost care, » and to this purpose « the *Scholae cantorum* are to be fostered... musical training and practice, *praxis musicae,* are to be greatly prized and looked to in seminaries, novitiates, houses of study, » etc.

Among the various kinds of sacred music, Gregorian chant has, of course, pride of place: « *Ecclesia cantum gregorianum agnoscit ut liturgiae ro-*

manae proprium » — the Church recognises Gregorian chant as the chant proper to the Roman
liturgy and therefore wills that in the action of the
liturgy it has pride of place. » Beside it — rather
than after it — sacred polyphony: *« Alia genera Musicae sacrae, praesertim vero polyphonia, in cele-
brandis divinis Officiis minime excluduntur »*; and
just how much the Church has these things at heart
Paul VI gave voice to in addressing three thousand
young people of France who had moved him by
their singing of a Gregorian pontifical Mass in St.
Peter's: « Maybe some of you are anxious as to the
future application of the Constitution on the Sacred Liturgy... Let these read again the pages of
the admirable text regarding sacred chant, and in
particular the words *the treasure of sacred music
shall be conserved and fostered with the utmost
care*, and We think that they will be reassured. »

We surely had the right to be. But what do
rights count for in these nightmare times of arrogance and subversion we are passing through?
Discomforted in Rome, the innovators hie to the
court of Felsina, there to think up a further « Instruction » to give themselves grounds once again
for forbidding what has been ordered, and ordering what has been forbidden.

Not long afterwards came your well-nigh incredible order, rigorously prescribed, for an *Italian
sung Mass*, by you denominated « Vatican II » (but
given a less magisterial and high-sounding name
by the people) to be learned and adopted by every
parish community, and for pontifical Masses *the
only one allowed*, in place of sung Mass in Gregorian. Of this masterpiece, your « Vatican II », a
Catholic musicologist — evidently no friend of
yours — wrote that it is a pretty beastly thing when
a parcel of jaundiced progressives, with a will to
make us swallow down doses of subhuman culture,

in an age of magnificent musical inventiveness
which even the masses are coming to appreciate
and like more, succeeds in foisting upon the faithful Christian people good-for-nothing stuff devoid
of musical form and content, just because the head
of the liturgical « reform » has high-handedly disposed, and imposed. »

« Music, I imagine, » Plato said, « ought to end
in the love of the Beautiful »; and Ruskin, remark-
ing on this, wrote: « The Greeks only called *Musica*
the kind of sound which induced right moral feel-
ling... and any other kind of sound than that... they
did not call Music (exercise under the Muses) but
Amusia — the denial or desolation for want of the
Muses. » *Amusia* of the lowest level I have no doubt
the Greeks, and the great English art critic and
lover of the Catholic liturgy (though no Catholic)
would have found your Italo-Catholic « Vatican II »
— Ruskin also writing in his autobiography,
« *Praeterita* », of his discovery that every manner of
Protestant written services whatsoever were either
« *insolently altered corruptions, or washed-out and
dragged-down rags and débris of the great Catholic
collects, litanies and songs of praise.* » If history
cannot really repeat itself, then historical situations certainly seem to, as we see now.

To quote a modern critic, in relation to the
5th international Church Music Congress held in
the U.S.A. in 1966, Fr Richard Schuler wrote in a
specialist ecclesiastical publication of that year:
« The very art of music in the liturgy is endanger-
ed by those promoting changes without the musi-
cianship to carry them through. This leads to
puritanism and iconoclasm in regard to musical
art... What is more, many fail to realise that the
desired « *actuosa participatio* » (of the Liturgical
Constitution) originates in the *baptismal character*, which gives the Christian his right to take part

in the Eucharistic Mysteries. This he does *by virtue of his Baptism;* and when he wills to worship, to offer the Victim and receive Communion, then he indeed « actively » takes part. This taking part is fostered by the externals of standing, kneeling, speaking, singing; but these are not in themselves « *actuosa participatio* », but rather means to help achieve it. Since the above term is the key-word of the Constitution, and the sum and substance of the present liturgical revival... to misunderstand it leads to the abuses of the Constitution that have resulted in some places, and to a downgrading of the art of music as well. »

There is also « active » taking part by *listening,* which is, Monsignor Blanchet, ex-director of the Paris Catholic Institute, has declared, « *often more effective than outward participation* ». In the 6th chapter of Isaiah — origin of the liturgical *Sanctus* — we read how the prophet, *listening to the song of the Seraphim,* was moved to the depths of his being with humility, the spirit of penitence and sense of God's majesty and mercy.

Part of the trouble has undoubtedly arisen from the mistranslation of the word « *actuosa* » as « active », by which has been understood external gestures, words, singing — *doing* something — such as one sees going on in our churches nowadays. The *participatio actuosa* required by the Council, and always required of the faithful in the greatest possible degree, is the *inward* concentration of the mind and heart on the Mystery in the Mass of Christ's death and Resurrection, the offering of the Sacrifice together with Christ, the Sole Priest, body and soul, for God's adoration, our salvation and the world's redemption. Such participation, even if offered mutely and without movement, is nonetheless a true and full participation. It even *requires* a certain silence, and stillness.

To come back to Plainsong, Plainchant, Gregorian and polyphony, this music has a dignity and simplicity hardly to be found in any other. The melodies are impersonal and spiritual, uplifting and purifying in their influence on man's heart. Springing from the very cadences of the Latin that inspired them, Gregorian chant is not music set to words, but words set to music. And now this most beautiful, most inspired and holy music of all time, against the words of the Pope and the will of the conciliar Constitution, you are intent on burying, substituting for it, in the name of the good of the people and Christian renewal, the ugly, uninspired and tasteless varietes of popular community singing. And worse things still are being done in regard to sacred music — things against nature — as it were boiling the kid in the mother's milk (forbidden in Genesis to the Hebrews): *the vernacular is being sung to Gregorian melody.* This the Church has positively and absolutely prohibited. « *Lingua cantus gregoriani est unice lingua latina* », declared Pius XII (*Documenta pontificia ad instaurationem liturgicam,* collected by Fr Bugnini himself, your Consilium Secretary), which John XXIII confirmed, saying « the Latin language is indissolubly linked to Gregorian melody, » and which the conciliar Constitution codified in article 91, sarcely contradicted by Paul VI when, at the consecration of the rebuilt Montecassino Abbey on October 24th 1964, the Pope appealed to the Benedictine family to be « the faithful and jealous custodians of the treasure of Catholic tradition, and above all the school and model of liturgical prayer in its purest forms, its true and sacred chant, and its traditional, noble Latin language... »

And here is what the late Benedictine Abbot of Beuron, Abbot Reetz, has left on record, in an article published in 1965: « It has been suggested

in various countries that the whole of the Liturgy
of the Word up to the Offertory should be in the
language of the people. This would clearly mean
that Gregorian chant... would completely disappear.
But we cannot and ought not to give up, for any
reason whatever, the precious treasure we have in
Latin and Gregorian. » Going on to quote a modern theologian, who maintains that the Latin Mass
has been one of the main reasons why millions of
workers have drifted away from the Church in the
past hundred years, Abbot Kleetz continues: « Have
not those Christian Churches that have been using
the vernacular for four hundred years lost workers
also?... We can find today many Catholic working
people, men and women and their families, who
remain entirely faithful to their religion. Until now,
a liturgy in the vernacular has rarely filled a church,
whereas the opposite is true of the liturgy celebrated
in Latin... » And concluding: « The Catholic
Church has always tried to unite the faithful
through a uniform liturgy; and the *fundamental
reason why she has succeeded* has been the using
of a single language and a single chant especially
suited to it... The same holds good today... »

How many, even knowledgeable persons, were
not long ago deceived and dismayed on reading in
a studious article purporting to be written by a
priest of the Vatican, quoting a certain Catholic
daily of Bologna, that Fr Antonio Rosmini, religious
philosopher and Founder, in his famous book (*)
re-published with the approval of the Doctrinal Congregation, describing one of the Church's wounds
as the barrier between priest and laity resulting
in the inability of the laity to participate effectively
in the sacred rites... « advocated the use of the
local language in the Mass as one of the ways to

(*) « *Five Wounds of the Church* ».

overcome such obstacles... » In Fr Rosmini's book, however, *no such advocacy is actually found* — in fact, the very opposite, the remedy being *to instruct the people.*

Anyway, your Eminence, after some of these vernacular-Gregorian Masses of your invention, I have heard with my own ears the derisive laughter of *the people*, their parodying of your pompous and excecrable parody — making one think of a crow strutting about in the moulting plumage of a peacock — or, to take a metaphor nearer home, a nightingale's trilling from the beak of a jay.

COCKS AND CAPONS

Pray in ugliness seems to be what you, and your disciples, have undertaken to make of St. Pius X's *pray in beauty;* and one has to persuade oneself to believe that your fanaticism and iconoclasm have been of upright intention, burning with pure and apostolic zeal, to prevent oneself thinking that Masonry has had a hand in these things. This would be quite in keeping with its well-known past tactics of fabricating and spreading a certain type of counterfeit pious card with no other intention than of casting discredit on true religion and piety.

Knowing how much the soul of man is influenced by all that strikes his senses, the Church has ever appealed to music, most spiritual of the arts. *Cantare amantis est* — we sing because we love — the Holy Father recently quoted St. Augustine, addressing the *Pueri Cantores;* and the Church's song, Gregorian, was made to give voice to no vague and nebulous thought and emotion. It was made to express, according to sound theological truth, acts of supernatural faith, hope, adoration and divine praise. Striking at this, the Roman Church's official and highest prayer in song, what have you done — to take a homely farmyard simile — but set about making cocks into capons: away with the crests, wattles and sundry appurtenances and let all quack and cluck like ducks and chickens! No more crowing, smacking of « triumphalism », or « estheticism » — that would be out of place in the community — assembly — even though a disciple who once denied the Master started at that cry and wept bitterly — even though the liturgy extol the cock in several places: « *Gallus iacentes excitat... Gallus negantes arguit... Gallo canente spes redit...* »

Neither does one thereby wish to deny to hens and ducks and geese any more than to crows, jackdaws and magpies their part and importance in the polyphony of creation — one only asks that there be not banished from the divine praise the voices of the cock, the nightingale, the blackbird, the song-thrush, the lark and the linnet, no fault of theirs God having given them a better larynx and more varied, finer utterance.

Not long ago I heard the *Missa Papae Marcelli* executed in Rome by the London Ambrosian Singers; and again in Florence by the Sistine Chapel choir. This Mass, five centuries old, reminded me — it was plain non-Catholics present felt it also — of what Paul VI told the members of the Berlin *Deutsche Oper* in 1965: that religious music was « *an ambassador of Christ.* »

« If they will not read the Gospel, » the late Monsignor Perosi used to say, « I shall give it them in music. » But you, your Eminence, first fulminating against Michaelangelo, Arnolfo, Bernini, Pugin and other architects of « non-functional » churches (not being able to demolish them or dispose of a local earthquake) then turn your attention to the casting out of Palestrina, Victoria, Bach and Haendel, to say nothing of the many other anonymous sacred composers who have so often, by their melodies and harmonies *ex auditu* helped lift souls to God more effectively than any spoken words...

« *Beauté sanctifiante* » — we make our own the phrase of the French poetess, Marie Noël, weeping over the ruin you have made — you and your « *clercs novateurs* », propagators of a religion of words (« *une religion discoureuse* ») — of what art, the handmaid of God, had created in His praise.

« Have these reformers, belated Calvinists », asks Marie Noël, « never paused to reflect upon the Gift, made to the masses, of this Catholic liturgy of ours, thanks to which the Church Militant, going by earthly ways, rests her feet for a few radiant instants on the bottom-most steps of the Church Triumphant in Heaven? — that Gift of the Church to her people *which the people well understand*. The manifold riches of the liturgy: the earthly and heavenly appeal of the Advent *Rorate;* the *Gloria, laus!*... burgeoning into the triumph of Palm Sunday; the *Exsultet* of the Easter Vigil; the triple Pascal *Alleluia;* the sigh from beyond the grave of the Office of the Dead, and its terrible, suppliant *Dies irae;* the *Parce, Domine* in the event of public calamity; the shining and supernatural epic of thanksgiving of the *Te Deum*... all this magnificent song the Catholic Church gives the people in the *unequalled equality* of her universal charity — to King and president as to the littlest of her little ones... The oft-repeated words of the *Veni Creator*, the *Miserere, De profundis, Magnificat* had become familar treasures, thanks to the munificence of the Catholic Church whose prayer of the centuries upraises and ennobles humble and ordinary folk unawares, more than the lessons and lectures of all times and places put together. ».

If we may add an observation of our own, it is that signs are already beginning to be seen. It has needed the removal of the Gift by blundering, plundering, harsh hands for the people to have become aware of it, appreciate it more. Your way, your Eminence, has certainly not been God's; but then God's ways are not ours...

Sacred music has in liturgical prayer pride of place of which only the deaf can be unaware. « If art, » an eminent composer has exclaimed, « is one of God's gifts to mankind, then the artist is as an instrument working, at times without realising it, above and beyond any kind of intellectualistic reasoning, and arriving where no one else is able to arrive. The Church's liturgy finds in music and chant *its very soul*... and above all in the Liturgy of Holy Week; for this has been the object of such sublime musical interpretation in the liturgy as to constitute a monument in itself of universal beauty. »

I should like to end this chapter with one last quotation from an author long loved throughout the world, Robert Louis Stevenson. Despite the present craze among Catholics for fault-finding in regard to their own religion, the true and perfect one, their predilection for flattering others that are imperfect or false, these remarks of Stevenson's will not be amiss, so appreciative are they of the spirit of the Roman liturgy, so frankly acknowledging what Protestantism lacks, himself no Catholic: after describing the old mission church, now gone to ruin, built by the Jesuits for the Californian Indians of Carmel, and how only once a year now a « padre » arrives to celebrate in the sacristy, only part of the church still standing, the story (*The Old Pacific Capital*) continues: « ...And there... you may hear God served with perhaps more touching circumstances that in any other temple under heaven. An Indian, stoneblind and about eighty years of age, conducts the singing; other Indians compose the choir; yet, they have the Gregorian music at their finger ends, and pronounce the Latin so correctly that I could follow the meaning as they sang. The pronunciation was odd and nasal, the singing hurried and staccato. « *In saecula saeculo-ho-ho-rum* », they went, with a vigorous aspirate to every additional syllable. I have never seen faces more vividly lit up with joy than the faces of these Indian singers. It was to them not only the worship of God, nor an act by which they recalled and commemorated better days, but was, besides, an exercise of culture, where all they knew of art and letters was united and expressed. And it made one's heart sorry for the good fathers of yore, who had taught them to dig and to reap, and to sing, who had given them European Mass books which they still preserve and study in their cottages, and who had now passed away from all authority and influence in that land — to be succeeded by greedy land-thieves and sacrilegious pistol-shots. So ugly a thing may our Anglo-Saxon Protestantism appear beside the doings of the Society of Jesus. »

THE PARISH CHOIR: A MEMORY

I took part as a member of the parish choir for the last time in Holy Week — but only in some of it — two years ago. The barrenness of the altars accentuated the forlorn and empty church interior, now more Protestant than Catholic, the insufficiency and wretchedness of the rickety ply-wood contraption in the middle of the aisle upon which, back to the Tabernacle (as yet unremoved) and altar, the priest had lately been obliged to make Our Lord come down into our midst — emptiness and desolation fitting enough for the liturgical time of year, but I mean of the whole liturgical era by you, your Eminence, ushered in.

The church was half deserted and it was as sad as it was embarrassing to hear the public scoldings of the priest for the people's no more being willing to lend him a hand (or even a foot, for none were forthcoming to take part in the *lavanda* ceremony, as formerly). How different all was from previous years, when, the choir as well filled as the nave, all the people took part, with lips and heart, singing or listening to the familiar ceremonies, known and loved from childhood — the Mattins, and Plainsong Lamentations, the four-part *Miserere*, the *Vexilla regis* and *Stabat Mater* that moved to tears and put one in mind of the Passion as much if not more than any « liturgy of the word », or sermon.

To be a member of the choir in country parts was once a coveted honour. Every parish had its choir and was very proud of it. No sacrifice was too great for its members, turning out at night for rehearsals, no matter if snow was on the ground or there was flooding, or if one's bones were aching with fatigue, or one had to put off a date with one's girl-friend, who as likely as not was also one of the singers... How wonderful were those sung Masses of ours! Coming out of church, the people would thank us and shower us with congratulations — and that was the only reward we had, or wanted, either, though there was the supper offered by the parish priest on Palm Sunday at the outset of Holy Week, and a glass of wine now and then at the end of evening ceremonies. One thing we always held to, and that was the Requiem Mass sung by us who remained for any that had passed on before... And as for me, my hope, as one-time member of the choir, is that when my time comes I too shall have that Mass, *in die obitus*... the one we often sang together for others in times past. I *hope*, I say, for by the time my sunset comes, may the sun once more have risen on different times!... I hope that my friends and former companion singers will make heard over my coffin those sublime and eternal sequences, like no other — the Church's own — and that there may never be heard a note of the grotesque, banal and shameful pieces we have lately had to hear...

How lovely were those sung Masses! How salutary and moving it was to sing those *Kyrie, Gloria, Credo* to melodies as old as the Church, composed by their authors on their knees, making us consequently kneel in belief, hope and love!... The comparison scarcely bears thinking on, so much grief it arouses, not to say indignation and disgust; for how deeply felt, as nothing else, those melodies were by the people you and your rationalists could have had no idea, with your plans, in conformity with a tendency of the age, to treat the Mass and other ceremonies not as sacred mysteries that elevate and sanctify hearts and minds able or willing to correspond, but as the public shows and cinemas made as accessible and as understandable as possible on the popular level to all. For centuries and centuries the Church, the Spouse of Christ, has had it as her constant desire to beautify and sanctify her churches, rites, vestments, song — and you, against the laws of popes and Councils, against tradition, the practice and teachings of saints, the love of the people, proceed to cast all away — *ut quid perditio haec?* — impoverishing, vulgarizing, proletarizing, taking away the queenly mantle, putting the Church in overalls, not fearing to be accused of Puritanism, nor disdaining the applause of Marxists for the « tremendous changes », the giving up of « triumphalist positions » and of the « Constantinian spirit », etc. etc.

And, through the same door by which Latin, Gregorian and sacred music have been shown out, there has been let in the language of the marketplace, together with every kind of common cacophany. Your restless, regimented, wordy liturgy is now crammed with sound, as one has written from Portugal, « like the house of the next door neighbour with its incessant pop tunes or talks blared or boomed from TV and radiogrammes... and the few moments of silence and recollection granted seem like the brief intervals of quiet between one record and another, or the pauses between the pounding of the juke-box in the bar.

Through the door by which Latin, Gregorian and sacred music have been thrust out, there have pushed their way in, with your encouragement — at your instigation, rather (as I said, one cannot avoid suspecting the Church's very enemies have had a hand) — hybrid Masses half in Latin, half in the common language (at one moment *Dominus vobiscum*, showing the people understand, the next *the Lord be with you!*, the two Latin words too difficult for them after all); amphibious Masses, sung a little in Latin, a little in the vernacular (to a kind of Plainchant); Gregorian-vernacular monstrosities; esperanto Masses; jazz Masses; yé-yé, twist, hootenanny Masses; Masses to the beat of the tom-tom and the sensuous wail of the mandoline and electric guitar; Parisian Puig Masses, imitated in Rome, accompanied, or rather noisified, by vibraphones and the hiss and grunt of percussion, provoking hoots of laughter from such members of the audience — one cannot say congregation — as did not rush out with their fingers in their ears, or shouting and shaking their fists against the profanation of holy rites and sacred precincts... To this your liturgical carnival has led. And when it seemed that this « experimentation » in « adaptation to the modern mentality » had reached such a pitch as made it impossible for this guinea-pig liturgy to suffer further, we found we were wrong: for within a mile of St. Peter's, aided and abetted by the members of a religious Order, we had (not celebrated, it was urged, *tried out,* only) a « Mass of the Beatles », with contortions and yellings. Some said they were not sure whether to call it « the Mass of the Madhouse » or « the Mass of the Brothel ». The music set to special « liturgical » texts including the « modified » Our Father adapted to electric guitars and amplifiers at full volume, not merely reduced to next to none the margin between the sacred and profane, but was pre-planned downright *profane* without any pretence whatever, the work of a filmscript composer, so as to enable girl participants in *Courrèges*, others in « op » outfits, to disport and contort themselves to « shake » rhythm, producing a pandemonium which scandalized and revolted all but the frenzied actors and a handful of fans — incredible to say, among these, some priests and nuns. Given a scornful reception unanimously by the daily papers, one or two « Catholic » ones ventured to opine that this was, after all, going a bit too far. Even the Italian Communist *Unità,* however, hazarded: « To be sure, the prospect of seeing the hundreds of Rome churches changed into so many Piper clubs is not entrancing. »

Yes, we have been going a bit too far, indeed... But as the monks of the middle ages, bent over their manuscripts in the seclusion of their monasteries, managed to preserve the treasures of both pagan Classicism and Christian doctrine for future generations, so today lay people are not lacking who, in the midst of the world, are exerting themselves in an effort to save what the Church's priests and religious, a-thirst for modernity and novelty, are in many cases foolishly scrapping or throwing overboard.

Even the 1967 Instruction on Sacred Music, *Musicam Sacram*, rather than remedy the sad plight in which sacred music finds itself, has only served to aggravate the situation; and according to the best musical critics and qualified judges it has still wider opened the door to every sort of arbitrariness, dispute and disagreement. It has been found « inadequate, even damaging, for its lack of coherence, and its contradictions »; it has been called « a compromise showing no homogenuity or clarity », contradictory in substance, taking us far indeed from the great liturgical documents of the past, the *motu proprio* of St. Pius X, the *Musicae sacrae disciplina* of Pius XII, and the *Iucunda laudatio* of John XXIII. » It is further deplorable, competent authorities say, that a document aiming to be of a purely executive character regarding a pre-existing law in force should introduce new norms and radical modifications. Once more, *but without its being evident to all*, new ways are opened up leading away from Gregorian and towards congregational singing in the everyday language, amounting to a negation and a profanation of sacred music. Monsignor Lavinio Virgilio, maestro of the Lateran pontifical choir, publicly expressing his dismay at the Instruction's encouragement of experimentation with new types of music during Mass, exclaims: « What must we make of this condescending approval of pointless and foolish experiments? Is it fitting to make the liturgy an object of experimentation? Is the liturgy rather not an act to which the fruits of mature deliberation and decision are to be made applicable? »

USQUEQUO, DOMINE?...

You have indeed, your Eminence, been « going a bit too far »... But even in this there is hope. *Deus, venerunt gentes in hereditatem tuam, polluerunt templum sanctum tuum... Usquequo, Domine?...* Many of us there are now — more and more — crying out and praying to God; and the more your innovating and destructive passion grows, the more will grow our hope that God will hear us, in the end.

It is comforting, then, to learn of this « going too far » — the evil coming principally, we are sure, from the Babel unloosed by the putting aside of the Church's unity of language, making way (as with every heretical trend) for all the rest — for the ravages of this neo-Modernist epidemic, compared with which that of the times of St. Pius X and his Secretary of State, the Servant of God, Cardinal Merry del Val (whose beatification is devoutly hoped for) was like an attack of hay fever — as Maritain has it, in *The Peasant of the Garonne*. The *doyen* of Catholic philosophy has clearly seen and described how the obscuring or whittling down of the distinction between the spiritual and the temporal has led to the natural world, before which many Christians now think necessary to kneel, being taken for the Mystical Body; and drawing on the observations of Cardinal Journet and Etienne Gilson he makes short work, too, of Teilhardism, the new world worshiping *religion of progress* and the « cosmic Christ », not without a charitable survey of Teilhard himself, to whom he ironically attributes a « great imagination ».

It is comforting, also, to know of the alarm of certain good Anglicans, reported a while ago by *The Times*, over certain ideas under discussion with the Church of Rome, which had always seemed an immovable rock, and, despite their not seeing eye to eye, a comforting one from its massive immobility and firm attachment to the ancient faith, whilst the world is shifting, no longer believing in anything definite at all. Comforting the envy of some Communists for our unity of language (what is left) and Communion; the non-Catholic artists' and intellectuals' envy of the beauties of our liturgy (if, as Paul VI has said, *it is still worthy of the name*) and of our Catholic art (where it has not been wrecked or thrown out of church). Comforting the hope afforded by so many young people, many of whom, from the little Latin they know or have studied, are increasingly aware, as de-Latinization progresses, of the vernacular's vulgarity and inadequacy which on Sunday all are obliged to hear — and many have had enough of it.

Children, too, providing they have not been corrupted, naturally feel it is nicer to pray in Latin. Parents and teachers can testify to this, the child's innocent soul at once able to perceive its mysterious beauty.

« The Church from earliest times, » Christine Mohrmann concludes her admirable study, *Liturgical Latin, Its Origins and Character,* « has felt herself closely united with the heavenly liturgy, and we may say that she seeks here already, in the form of her liturgy, what St. Augustine termed « praising Thee with one voice, and being made one in Thee

— *laudantes te in unum, et in te facti unum »* (*De Trinitate*).

Our comfort is in these things. Our *hope* is in the universal agreement of simple and humble persons, children and people, in the Church's saints and doctors, and in the unequivocal pronouncements of the Servants of God, Pius XII and John XXIII.

Our hope is in Paul VI's proclamation of Our Lady *Mater Ecclesiae*, Mother of the Church, to whom we steadfastly pray with boundless love and trust, fearing no excess, as some do today, but Dante and St. Bernard did not:

> *Lady, so great art thou and such thy might*
> *The seeker after grace who shuns thy knee*
> *May aim his prayer, but fails to wing his flight* (***).

Mary, Mother of the Church, Queen and Mother — *electa ut Sol, terribilis ut castrorum acies* — she who « cometh forth as the morning rising, fair as the moon, bright as the sun, terrible as an army set in battle array », as the Church extols her, the exterminator of every error and heresy: *cunctas haereses sola interemisti*.

Mary, Mother of the Church, *Mater Ecclesiae* — as it fell to Paul VI to proclaim her, placing one jewel more in her Crown, just as the new Modernism, as the pontiff discerned and affirmed in *Ecclesiam suam*, was insinuating itself again within the one true fold, attenuating Marian doctrine and

---

(*) « The Divine Comedy », *Paradise*, XXXIII, 13,15 (Trans. Dorothy L. Sayers and Barbara Reynolds. Penguin Books 1966).

devotion, endeavouring to dim the Virgin's glorious lustre:

Then still within my sight they lingered, singing
Regina coeli *with such dulcet sound*
Within me still the joy of it is ringing.

O what a fertile yield doth there abound,
Oerflowing from rich coffers which of old
On earth were acres of good seeding-ground!

There life they have, and on that wealth take hold
In Babylonian exile dearly won,
In tears and sorrow, caring nought for gold.

There too, victorious, beneath the Son
Of God and Mary, amid the consistory
Of Councils new and ancient, triumphs one

Who holds the keys of such celestial glory (*).

Our *certainty* is in her.

To the Church Triumphant and the Church Expiating in the Holy Souls in Purgatory there will never be lacking the prayers and hymns of the Church Militant, daily and from all the altars of the world renewing faith, hope, charity, thanksgiving and praise...

Cum quibus et nostras voces ut admitti iubeas... And so that this voice of ours, the least worthy, may be acceptable, I end by begging you to help with our prayers the writer who, for love of the Church's language and liturgy, may have caused you pain, your Eminence.

(*) Ibid. XXIII, 127-139. *In the Celestial Rose, St. Peter is seen sitting on the right hand of the Virgin* (XXXII, 124-26) among the saints from the Old and New Dispensation.

APPENDIX

SACRIFICIUM LAUDIS: the Apostolic Letter of His Holiness Paul VI to Superiors General of Religious Communities bound to the recitation of Divine Office in Choir.

The sacrifice of praise, offered by those professed to faith in the Lord, the psalmody and chant whereby are sanctified the hours, days and seasons of the year, centred in the Eucharistic Sacrifice, as the shining of the noonday sun attracting all things to itself, have by uninterrupted custom ever been held in greatest consideration by your religious communities, vowed to the divine service.

Rightly indeed was it believed that nothing should come before so holy a religious practice. It is then easily understandable how much glory has been thereby given to God our Creator and how much utility has resulted for the Church.

By means, therefore, of this form of prayer, established and maintained perpetually through the centuries, you have taught that divine worship is of supreme importance in human society.

But, from the letters We have been receiving from some among you, also various missives reaching Us from others, We have come to know that the Religious Houses or Provinces depending on you — We speak of those of the Latin rite only — have been adopting different customs in the celebration of the sacred liturgy: whilst for some, on the one hand, the Latin language may not be interfered with, others, nevertheless, are asking for the vernacular languages and, still further, for the chant known as Gregorian to be here and there replaced by popular ditties in vogue today. By some it is claimed outright that the Latin language should be done away with.

We confess that requests of this kind have gravely disturbed and not a little grieved Us; and the question puts itself, where ever did this widespread frame of mind and hitherto unheard of insufferance arise, and why it has been spread abroad.

You certainly are aware, and cannot doubt, how much We have at heart, and what great store We set by, your religious communities. Many and admirable are the examples of outstanding piety and civic virtues that have given them lustre and fame. And it is a great joy to have offered Us the occasion to act on their behalf and uphold their desires — so long as lawful and suitable things are concerned — and provide for their happier estate.

But the things We have denounced above are taking place after the Second Vatican Council has expressly and solemnly pronounced upon the matter (Cf. Const. Lit. 101, I) and after clear and precise rulings have been issued in relative Instructions. In one of these issued for the disciplining of the Constitution's practical applications in regard to the Sacred Liturgy, on September 26th 1964, this was decreed: « In the recitation of the Divine Office in Choir the clergy are bound to preserve the Latin language (no. 85). In another Instruction entitled « Of the language to be used in the celebration of the Divine Office, etc., » bearing date of publication November 23rd 1965, the same obligation is reconfirmed and at the same time the reason adduced of the spiritual advantage of the faithful, as well as of particular conditions that may prevail for regions having to be cultivated by missionary activity.

Until such time, then, as anything different shall be lawfully laid down, these are the laws in force, requiring that obedience which it is above all needful for the members of religious communities, the Church's most dear sons, to be distinguished by.

Nor, furthermore, is it here but a question of the preservation of the Latin language in the recitation of the Divine Office in Choir — language which, far from being held in little honour is certainly worthy of lively defence, it being in the Latin Church the most fertile source of Christian civilisation and richest treasure of piety — but it is also a question of keeping intact the decorum, beauty and original vigour of these prayers and chants: it is a question, that is to say, of the Divine Office's being sung in Choir with those « notes of the Church, which she sweetly sings » (Cf. St. Aug. Conf. 9,6; PL 32,796) which your Founders and masters and saints in heaven, luminaries of your Families, have handed down to you. Not to be held of little account are those things which the Fathers instituted, and which for long centuries afforded you lustre and fame. Moreover, this manner of reciting the Divine

Office in Choir has been one of the main reasons why your very religious Families remained united and welded together, enjoying happy growth, and increase. It therefore gives rise to astonishment that, shaken by sudden storms, this manner of prayer seems to some by now something that may be set aside.

In the existing condition of things, what language, what chant is able to take the place of these forms of Catholic piety that have up to now served you in good stead? It is necessary to reflect and watch lest a worse situation arise, if once that glorious inheritance were rejected. The danger is that the choral Office be reduced to a bare recitation which you would be the first to feel the poorer for, and which could produce tedium.

There is also this problem: would those desirous of hearing the holy chants and prayers continue to frequent your churches in such numbers when there were no more heard there to resound that immemorial and original language of theirs joined to a chant so full of gravity and fitting beauty?

We therefore ask all responsible and concerned to weigh well what it is they are wishing to get rid of, and not to let the springs from which they have freely drawn till now run dry.

Without doubt, Latin may afford the novices of your holy militia some hardship, not light, perhaps. But this, as you know, is not such as cannot be conquered or overcome, especially in your Houses where, farther removed from the cares and noise of the world, you may the more easily give yourselves to the study of letters.

For the rest, these prayers so full of strength and noble majesty will continue to attract to you young people called to the service of God; the choir, on the contrary, that were to be deprived of that language, which is above the boundaries of individual nations and whose worth is in its wonderful spiritual force — the choir that were to eliminate those melodies rising up from the depths of the soul — We mean Gregorian Chant — would be like a snuffed candle, giving light no more, no more drawing men's minds and gaze.

However, dearest sons, the requests above referred to are of such grave moment that for the present it is not possible for Us to grant them, derogating from the Council's norms and those of the above-recalled Instructions.

We exhort you, then, with all Our strength, to ponder

111

well and long, and as to its every aspect, a matter so delicate and complex.

We do not wish, for the love We have for you and the great esteem that is Ours, to grant what could bring about a worsening, and be the origin, possibly, of no small harm to yourselves, as well of undoubted weakening and sorrow for the whole Church of God. Allow Us to protect your heritage, even inspite of yourselves.

From the Church herself, who, for reasons of pastoral utility, and for the convenience of the people not knowing Latin, has introduced the use of vernacular languages into the Sacred Liturgy, you now receive the mandate to conserve — both as regards language and chant — the traditional dignity, the beauty and gravity of the choral Office.

Meanwhile, therefore, obey with sincere and tranquil spirit these precepts which no outmoded love for ancient customs but rather Our paternal love for you suggests, and which your own zeal for divine worship persuades you to.

Finally, as conciliator of heavenly gifts and testimony of our benevolent regard, We impart to you and your brethren, with all our heart in the Lord, Our Apostolic Blessing.

Given in Rome, at St. Peter's, on August 15th, Feast of the Assumption of the Blessed Virgin Mary, in the year 1966, the IV of Our Pontificate.

PAULUS PP. VI

www.ingramcontent.com/pod-product-compliance
Lightning Source LLC
Chambersburg PA
CBHW022011090426
42741CB00007B/985

*9 7 8 1 6 2 1 3 8 6 4 3 8 *